STANDARD METHOD OF MEASUREMENT OF BUILDING WORKS

SEVENTH EDITION

AMENDMENT 2

Page	Rule	Correction
22	A52.1	Insert new Coverage Rule 'C1 Fixing only such items is deemed to include unloading, storing, hoisting the goods and materials and returning packaging materials to the nominated supplier carriage paid and obtaining credits therefor.'
		Insert new Supplementary Information Rule 'S1 Particulars of any costs to be paid of conveying goods and materials to the site and/or of any special packing or similar requirements.'
52	D1	Insert additional sentence at start of Rule 'Cast-in accessories include anchor bolts, anchor boxes, anchor fixing bolts, etc., dowels, column guards and isolated glass lenses.'
73	M2	Delete the words 'except in staircase areas.'
88	C4	Insert the word 'and' after 'crosses' in the second line and delete the words 'and trimming to openings.'
	6	Insert new Definition Rule 'D5 Abutments include trimming to openings which extend full height, full girth or full width, unless finished with the same finish as the faces. Trimming to openings which are not full height, full girth or full width are deemed to be included.'
89	8	Insert new Definition Rule 'D6 Fair ends to partitions include trimming to openings.'
	D5	Renumber as D7.
	D6	Renumber as D8.
105	17–22**7	Delete the words 'weathered tops.'
142	M5	For 'P30' read 'P30/31.'
175	M2(b)	For '0.50 m' read '0.60 m.'

Note: These amendments cover correction of typographical errors and minor textual alterations to achieve compatibility with the wording of JCT Contracts

May 1989

STANDARD METHOD OF MEASUREMENT OF BUILDING WORKS
SEVENTH EDITION
AMENDMENT 3

Page	Rule	Correction
18	1.*0.1	Delete the word 'seal' and insert the word 'deed'
33	1. & 2.*3	Delete rule 3 and insert new rule 3 'Total bored or driven length, maximum length stated'
	M1	Delete the word 'depths' in the second line and insert the word 'lengths'
	C1	Delete the words 'The work' in the first line and insert the words 'Total concrete length'
65	1.1–5.*	Insert new rules in third column '1 Weight ≤ 40 kg/m 2 Weight 40–100 kg/m 3 Weight > 100 kg/m'
	1.1–8.**	Insert new rule after 4 '5 Hollow, shape stated'
	M1	Delete the words 'and fittings except fittings of a different type and grade of material' in the second to fifth lines and insert the words 'except fittings'
	M2	Delete rule M2 and insert new rule M2 'Fittings are all grouped together irrespective of the member to which they are attached'
66	5.1	Insert the words 'use stated' after 'Plain member'
	5.2	Insert the words 'use and details of construction stated' after 'Built-up member'
	5.*	Insert horizontal line in second column below rule 2
	5.*	Insert new rule after 2 '3 Fittings'
	5.**	Delete rule 1, delete horizontal line between rules 1 and 2, delete rule 2 Insert new rules in third column '1 Weight ≤ 40 kg/m 2 Weight 40–100 kg/m 3 Weight > 100 kg/m'
	5.**	Insert horizontal line in third column below new rule 3
	5.***	Insert new rule after 4 '5 Hollow, shape stated'
	5.***	Insert horizontal line in fourth column below new rule 5
	D7	Delete the reference '1.10' in the second line and insert the reference '1.9'
	5	Insert new Coverage Rule 'C2 Isolated structural members are deemed to include fabrication and erection'
165	19.2	Insert the words 'type of' in the third line between 'and' and 'conduit'

Note: In conjunction with the major revisions to Section G10, 11 and 12 noted above the commentary on particular rules for this section in the SMM7 Measurement Code has been expanded.

May 1992

Standard Method of Measurement of Building Works

smm7

Standard Method of Measurement of Building Works

Authorised by agreement between the Royal Institution of Chartered Surveyors and the Building Employers Confederation

Co-ordinated project information

First Edition, 1922
Second Edition, 1927
Third Edition, 1935
Fourth Edition, 1948
Fifth Edition, 1963; amended 1964; metric 1968
Sixth Edition, 1979
Seventh Edition, 1988

Reprinted 1989
incorporating Amendment Sheets Nos 1 and 2
dated September 1988 and May 1989.

Reprinted 1992
incorporating Amendment Sheets Nos 1, 2 and 3
dated September 1988, May 1989 and May 1992.

Copyright   The Royal Institution of Chartered Surveyors
© 1988   The Building Employers Confederation

ISBN 0 85406 360 9 (RICS)
ISBN 0 85263 0004 3 (BEC)

Designed and set by NBS Services Ltd, Newcastle upon Tyne

Printed by Eyre & Spottiswoode, Margate, Kent.

Summary of contents

To find the relevant work section for any given topic refer to the detailed contents list overleaf or to the alphabetical index.

Detailed contents

H Cladding/Covering

J Waterproofing

K Linings/Sheathing/Dry partitioning

★ No specific rules included – see General rules clause 11.

R Disposal systems

R10	Rainwater pipework/gutters	141
R11	Foul drainage above ground	141
R12	Drainage below ground	145
R13	Land drainage	145
R14	Laboratory/Industrial waste drainage	Y
R20	Sewage pumping	Y
R21	Sewage treatment/sterilisation	Y
R30	Centralised vacuum cleaning	Y
R31	Refuse chutes	Y
R32	Compactors/Macerators	Y
R33	Incineration plant	Y

S Piped supply systems

S10	Cold water	Y
S11	Hot water	Y
S12	Hot and cold water (small scale)	Y
S13	Pressurised water	Y
S14	Irrigation	Y
S15	Fountains/Water features	Y
S20	Treated/Deionised/Distilled water	Y
S21	Swimming pool water treatment	Y
S30	Compressed air	Y
S31	Instrument air	Y
S32	Natural gas	Y
S33	Liquid petroleum gas	Y
S34	Medical/Laboratory gas	Y
S40	Petrol/Oil–lubrication	Y
S41	Fuel oil storage/distribution	Y
S50	Vacuum	Y
S51	Steam	Y
S60	Fire hose reels	Y
S61	Dry risers	Y
S62	Wet risers	Y
S63	Sprinklers	Y
S64	Deluge	Y
S65	Fire hydrants	Y
S70	Gas fire fighting	Y
S71	Foam fire fighting	Y

T Mechanical heating/Cooling/ Refrigeration systems

T10	Gas/Oil fired boilers	Y
T11	Coal fired boilers	Y
T12	Electrode/Direct electric boilers	Y
T13	Packaged steam generators	Y
T14	Heat pumps	Y
T15	Solar collectors	Y
T16	Alternative fuel boilers	Y
T20	Primary heat distribution	Y
T30	Medium temperature hot water heating	Y
T31	Low temperature hot water heating	Y
T32	Low temperature hot water heating (small scale)	Y
T33	Steam heating	Y
T40	Warm air heating	Y
T41	Warm air heating (small scale)	Y
T42	Local heating units	Y
T50	Heat recovery	Y
T60	Central refrigeration plant	Y
T61	Primary/Secondary cooling distribution	Y
T70	Local cooling units	Y
T71	Cold rooms	Y
T72	Ice pads	Y

Y: See Y Mechanical and electrical services measurement

U Ventilation/Air conditioning systems

Code	Description	
U10	General supply/extract	Y
U11	Toilet extract	Y
U12	Kitchen extract	Y
U13	Car parking extract	Y
U14	Smoke extract/Smoke control	Y
U15	Safety cabinet/Fume cupboard extract	Y
U16	Fume extract	Y
U17	Anaesthetic gas extract	Y
U20	Dust collection	Y
U30	Low velocity air conditioning	Y
U31	VAV air conditioning	Y
U32	Dual-duct air conditioning	Y
U33	Multi-zone air conditioning	Y
U40	Induction air conditioning	Y
U41	Fan-coil air conditioning	Y
U42	Terminal re-heat air conditioning	Y
U43	Terminal heat pump air conditioning	Y
U50	Hybrid system air conditioning	Y
U60	Free standing air conditioning units	Y
U61	Window/Wall air conditioning units	Y
U70	Air curtains	Y

V Electrical supply/power lighting systems

Code	Description	
V10	Electricity generation plant	Y
V11	HV supply/distribution/public utility supply	Y
V12	LV supply/public utility supply	Y
V20	LV distribution	Y
V21	General lighting	Y
V22	General LV power	Y
V30	Extra low voltage supply	Y
V31	DC supply	Y
V32	Uninterrupted power supply	Y
V40	Emergency lighting	Y
V41	Street/Area/Flood lighting	Y
V42	Studio/Auditorium/Arena lighting	Y
V50	Electric underfloor heating	Y
V51	Local electric heating units	Y
V90	General lighting and power (small scale)	Y

W Communications/Security/Control systems

Code	Description	
W10	Telecommunications	Y
W11	Staff paging/location	Y
W12	Public address/Sound amplification	Y
W13	Centralized dictation	Y
W20	Radio/TV/CCTV	Y
W21	Projection	Y
W22	Advertising display	Y
W23	Clocks	Y
W30	Data transmission	Y
W40	Access control	Y
W41	Security detection and alarm	Y
W50	Fire detection and alarm	Y
W51	Earthing and bonding	Y
W52	Lightning protection	Y
W53	Electromagnetic screening	Y
W60	Monitoring	Y
W61	Central control	Y
W62	Building automation	Y

X Transport systems

Code	Description	
X10	Lifts	149
X11	Escalators	149
X12	Moving pavements	149
X20	Hoists	149
X21	Cranes	149
X22	Travelling cradles	149
X23	Goods distribution/Mechanised warehousing	149
X30	Mechanical document conveying	149
X31	Pneumatic document conveying	149
X32	Automatic document filing and retrieval	149

Y: See Y Mechanical and electrical services measurement

Y Mechanical and electrical services measurement

Additional rules – work to existing buildings

Appendices

Alphabetical index

Preface to Seventh Edition 1988

The Joint Working Party on Measurement Conventions set up by The Royal Institution of Chartered Surveyors and the then National Federation of Building Trades Employers reported in December 1971. Out of this report a Development Unit was set up and quickly came to the conclusion that far reaching changes were required. As an interim measure the Sixth Edition of the Standard Method of Measurement was published in March 1979. Now, with the publication of this Seventh Edition, the work envisaged by that working party has been completed.

The Co-ordinating Committee for Project Information has produced a Common Arrangement of Work Sections for Building Works. In support of the principles of CCPI and in accordance with the wishes of the sponsoring bodies, this Edition has been structured in common arrangement order rather than in traditional work sections. This means that the Standard Method of Measurement is now compatible with other CCPI publications and with all standard documentation where these criteria have been adopted.

The other major change from previous editions is that the measurement rules have been translated from prose into classification tables. This change makes the use of the rules a quicker and more systematic task than interpretation of a prose version and readily lends itself to the use of standard phraseology and computerisation. The change however does not inhibit the use of traditional prose in the writing of bills of quantities if so desired. In addition to these two major changes, the rules have generally been simplified and the document brought up to date to equate with modern practice.

The Committee expresses its thanks to the professional and trade associations for their co-operation and advice in the detailed consultations that have taken place and to the surveyors and builders who have assisted in testing the new rules, to Geoffrey E. Beard who chaired the Committee from June 1975 to September 1984 and especially to the editors who have had the task of bringing together all the various drafts and presenting them in a uniform manner in a relatively short space of time.

This Seventh Edition will become operative on 1 July 1988 and is post dated accordingly.

The Joint Committee responsible for this edition at the date of issue was composed as follows:

Appointed by the Royal Institution of Chartered Surveyors: Christopher J. Willis (Chairman), Ronald C. Allan, Keith W. Bailey, John Bennett, Eric J. Bowman, N. Malcolm S. Boyd, Michael A. Rainbird, Eric H. Urquhart and Michael J.T. Webb.

Appointed by the Building Employers Confederation: Andrew J. Costelloe (Vice-Chairman), John M. Allen, Bernard Ball, Kenneth G. Ellis, James E. Fisher, Colin M. Ford, Richard J. Hooker, Robert H. Inglis, Terence J. Parkinson and Donald J. Rimmer.

Co-opted from the Development Unit: Tony Allott, Stuart Hendy, Peter E. Holden, Peter G. Jordan and Rex H. Sharman.

Consultant Members of the Committee: Geoffrey E. Beard and Ian M.C. Hill.

Joint Honorary Secretaries: Norman R. Wheatley (General) and Michael B. Smith (Queries).

Others who have served on the Committee or the Development Unit during the preparation of this edition: Dr Martin Barnes, Robert A. Barrow, Ian T. Brown, Peter Graham, Alan M. Harrison, Patrick Kelly, Anthony R. Miller and Paul D. Morrell.

Consultant Editors appointed by the Committee: Paul J. Gilkes and Richard E.N. McGill

CJW: 1 October 1987

Preface to First Edition 1922

For many years the Surveyors' Institution and the Quantity Surveyors' Association (which bodies are now amalgamated) were accepted as the recognised authorities for deciding disputed points in connection with the measurement of building works. The frequency of the demands upon their services for this purpose directed attention to the diversity of practice, varying with local custom, and even the idiosyncrasies of individual surveyors, which obtained. This lack of uniformity afforded a just ground of complaint on the part of contractors that the estimator was frequently left in doubt as to the true meaning of items in the bills of quantities which he was called upon to price, a circumstance which militated against scientific and accurate tendering.

In the absence of any statutory qualifications for surveyors practising in the United Kingdom, any person, up to the present, has been at liberty to describe himself as a quantity surveyor, and the public have no guarantee that he is qualified for that office. This fact resulted in the issue of a considerable amount of unskilled work under the designation of bills of quantities.

Both the Surveyors' Institution and the Quantity Surveyors' Association were impressed with the necessity of securing greater accuracy of work and uniformity of method. The latter body, in July 1909, with this object in view appointed a Committee who prepared and published pamphlets setting out the method of measurement recommended by the Association in respect of three trades. The Surveyors' Institution also issued to its members circulars giving an authoritative opinion as to the correct method of measurement in the case of items in connection with which disputes had occurred. The

desirability of co-operation between the two societies thus became evident, and a Joint Committee was set up in June 1912, upon which was imposed the task of drawing up a comprehensive set of Standard Rules of Measurement of Building Works. In 1918 representatives of the building trades were added to this Committee, four contractors being nominated by the National Federation of Building Trades Employers and the Institute of Builders. The Joint Committee were assisted in their deliberations by interviews with the representatives of certain trades.

The Standard Method of Measurement of Building Works drawn up and set forth in the following pages is founded upon the practice of the leading London quantity surveyors with certain modifications by way of alternatives, and not involving matters of principle, to suit the practice obtaining in other parts of the Kingdom.

The Joint Committee was composed as follows: six surveyors nominated by the Surveyors' Institution and the Quantity Surveyors' Association, and four contractors nominated by the National Federation of Building Trades Employers and the Institute of Builders, viz. Surveyors: Messrs. F.A.H. Hardcastle (Chairman), Thomas E. Bare (Hon.Sec.), R.C. Gleed, Arnold E. Harris, Walter Lawrence, and Morgan H. Young. Contractors: Messrs. R. Friend (Rugby) (Vice-Chairman), W. Lacey (London), Stanley Miller (Newcastle-on-Tyne) and Frank Woods (Bolton, Lancashire).

Other gentlemen who have served on the Committee for a time are: Surveyors: Messrs. Arthur G. Cross, W.E. Davis, J.E. Drower, and Henry Riley. Contractor: Mr. Walter Lawrence (London).

General rules

1. Introduction

1.1
This Standard Method of Measurement provides a uniform basis for measuring building works and embodies the essentials of good practice. Bills of quantities shall fully describe and accurately represent the quantity and quality of the works to be carried out. More detailed information than is required by these rules shall be given where necessary in order to define the precise nature and extent of the required work.

1.2
The rules apply to measurement of proposed work and executed work.

2. Use of the tabulated rules

Generally

2.1
The rules in this document are set out in tables. Each section of the rules comprises information (to be) provided, classification tables and supplementary rules. The tabulated rules are written in the present tense.

2.2
Horizontal lines divide the classification table and supplementary rules into zones to which different rules apply.

Classification tables

2.3
Within the classification table where a broken line is shown, the rules given above and below the broken line may be used as alternatives.

2.4
In referring to columns in classification tables the measurement unit column has been disregarded.

2.5
The left hand column of the classification table lists descriptive features commonly encountered in building works. The next column lists further sub-groups into which each main group of items shall be divided and similarly the third column provides for further division. The lists in these columns are not intended to be exhaustive.

2.6
Each item description shall identify the work with respect to one descriptive feature drawn from each of the first three columns in the classification table and as many of the descriptive features in the fourth column as are applicable to the item. The general principle does not apply to Preliminaries in that it will be necessary to select as many descriptive features as appropriate from each column.

2.7
Where the abbreviation (nr) is given in the classification table the quantity shall be stated in the item description.

Supplementary rules

2.8
Within the supplementary rules everything above the horizontal line, which is immediately below the classification table heading, is applicable throughout that table.

2.9
Measurement rules set out when work shall be measured and the method by which quantities shall be computed.

2.10
Definition rules define the extent and limits of the work represented by a word or expression used in the rules and in a bill of quantities prepared in accordance with the rules.

2.11
Coverage rules draw attention to particular incidental work which shall be deemed to be included in the appropriate items in a bill of quantities to the extent that such work is included in the tender documents. Where the coverage rules include materials they shall be mentioned in the item descriptions.

2.12
The column headed Supplementary Information contains rules governing the information which shall be given in addition to the information given as a result of the application of rule 2.6.

2.13
A separate item shall be given for any work which differs from other work with respect to any matter listed as supplementary information.

3. Quantities

3.1
Work shall be measured net as fixed in position except where otherwise stated in a measurement rule applicable to the work.

3.2
Dimensions used in calculating quantities shall be taken to the nearest 10mm (i.e. 5mm and over shall be regarded as 10mm and less than 5mm shall be disregarded).

3.3
Quantities measured in tonnes shall be given to two places of decimals. Other quantities shall be given to the nearest whole unit except that any quantity less than one unit shall be given as one unit.

3.4
Unless otherwise stated, where minimum deductions for voids are dealt with in this document they shall refer only to openings or wants which are within the boundaries of measured areas. Openings or wants which are at the boundaries of measured areas shall always be the subject of deduction irrespective of size.

3.5
The requirement to measure separate items for widths not exceeding a stated limit shall not apply where these widths are caused by voids.

4. Descriptions

4.1
Dimensions shall be stated in descriptions generally in the sequence length, width, height. Where ambiguity could arise, the dimensions shall be identified.

4.2
Information required by the application of rules 2.6 and 2.12 may be given in documents (e.g. drawings or specification) separate from the bills of quantities if a precise and unique cross reference is given in its place in the description of the item concerned. This rule does not allow the aggregation of a number of measured items which are otherwise required to be measured separately by these rules, except as provided by rule 9.1.

4.3
Headings to groups of items in a bill of quantities shall be read as part of the descriptions of the items to which the headings apply.

4.4
The use of a hyphen between two dimensions in this document or in a bill of quantities shall mean a range of dimensions exceeding the first dimension stated but not exceeding the second.

4.5
Each work section of a bill of quantities shall begin with a description stating the nature and location of the work unless evident from the drawn or other information required to be provided by these rules.

4.6
Unless otherwise specifically stated in a bill of quantities or herein, the following shall be deemed to be included with all items:

(a) Labour and all costs in connection therewith.
(b) Materials, goods and all costs in connection therewith.
(c) Assembling, fitting and fixing materials and goods in position.
(d) Plant and all costs in connection therewith.
(e) Waste of materials.
(f) Square cutting.
(g) Establishment charges, overhead charges and profit.

4.7
A dimensioned description for an item in the bill of quantities shall define the item and state all the dimensions necessary to identify the shape and size of the item or its components.

5. Drawn information

5.1
Location drawings:

(a) Block Plan: shall identify the site and locate the outlines of the building works in relation to a town plan or other context.

(b) Site Plan: shall locate the position of the building works in relation to setting out points, means of access and general layout of the site.

(c) Plans, Sections and Elevations: shall show the position occupied by the various spaces in a building and the general construction and location of the principal elements.

5.2
Component drawings: shall show the information necessary for manufacture and assembly of a component.

5.3
Dimensioned diagrams: shall show the shape and dimensions of the work covered by an item and may be used in a bill of quantities in place of a dimensioned description, but not in place of an item otherwise required to be measured.

5.4
Schedules which provide the required information shall be deemed to be drawings as required under these rules.

6. Catalogued or standard components

6.1
A precise and unique cross-reference to a catalogue or to a standard specification may be given in an item description instead of the description required by rules 2.6 and 2.12 or instead of a component drawing.

7. Work of special types

7.1
Work of each of the following special types shall be separately identified:

(a) Work on or in existing building – see general rule 13.

(b) Work to be carried out and subsequently removed (other than temporary works).

(c) Work outside the curtilage of the site.

(d) Work carried out in or under water shall be so described stating whether canal, river or sea water and (where applicable) the mean Spring levels of high and low water.

(e) Work carried out in compressed air shall be so described stating the pressure and the method of entry and exit.

8. Fixing, base and background

8.1
Method of fixing shall only be measured and described where required by the rules in each Work Section. Where fixing through vulnerable materials is required to be identified, such materials are deemed to include those listed in rule 8.3 (e).

8.2
Where the nature of the base is required to be identified each type of base shall be identified separately.

8.3
Where the nature of the background is required to be identified the item description shall state one of the following:

(a) Timber, which shall be deemed to include manufactured building boards.

(b) Masonry, which shall be deemed to include concrete, brick, block and stone.

(c) Metal.

(d) Metal faced materials.

(e) Vulnerable materials, which shall be deemed to include glass, marble, mosaic, tiled finishes and the like.

9. Composite items

9.1
Notwithstanding the requirement of clause 4.2, work to be manufactured off site may be combined into one item even though the rules require items to be measured separately, provided the items in question are all incorporated into the composite item off site. The item description shall identify the resulting composite item and the item shall be deemed to include breaking down for transport and installation and subsequent re-assembly.

13

10. Procedure where the drawn and specification information required by these rules is not available

10.1
Where work can be described and given in items in accordance with these rules but the quantity of work required cannot be accurately determined, an estimate of the quantity shall be given and identified as an approximate quantity.

10.2
Where work cannot be described and given in items in accordance with these rules it shall be given as a Provisional Sum and identified as for either defined or undefined work as appropriate.

10.3
A Provisional Sum for defined work is a sum provided for work which is not completely designed but for which the following information shall be provided:

(a) The nature and construction of the work.

(b) A statement of how and where the work is fixed to the building and what other work is to be fixed thereto.

(c) A quantity or quantities which indicate the scope and extent of the work.

(d) Any specific limitations and the like identified in Section A35.

10.4
Where Provisional Sums are given for defined work the Contractor will be deemed to have made due allowance in programming, planning and pricing Preliminaries. Any such allowance will only be subject to adjustment in those circumstances where a variation in respect of other work measured in detail in accordance with the rules would give rise to adjustment.

10.5
A Provisional Sum for undefined work is a sum provided for work where the information required in accordance with rule 10.3 cannot be given.

10.6
Where Provisional Sums are given for undefined work the Contractor will be deemed not to have made any allowance in programming, planning and pricing Preliminaries.

11. Work not covered

11.1
Rules of measurement adopted for work not covered by these rules shall be stated in a bill of quantities. Such rules shall, as far as possible, conform with those given in this document for similar work.

12. Symbols and abbreviations

12.1
The following symbols and abbreviations are used in this method of measurement:

m	=	metre
m²	=	square metre
m³	=	cubic metre
mm	=	millimetre
nr	=	number
kg	=	kilogramme
t	=	tonne
h	=	hour
p c sum	=	Prime Cost Sum
prov sum	=	Provisional Sum
>	=	exceeding
≥	=	equal to or exceeding
≤	=	not exceeding
<	=	less than
%	=	percentage
–	=	hyphen (see rule 4.4)

12.2

Cross references within the classification tables are given in the form:

Work Section number	:	Number from first column	.	Number from second column	.	Number from third column	.	Number from fourth column

Example:

D20: 2. 2. 2. 1

Excavation and filling

    Excavating

        To reduce levels

            Maximum depth ≤ 1.00m

            Commencing level stated where > 0.25m below existing ground level.

12.3

An asterisk within a cross reference represents all entries in the column in which it appears.

12.4

The digit 0 within a cross reference represents no entries in the column in which it appears.

13. Work to existing buildings

13.1

Work to existing buildings shall be so described. Such work is defined as work on, or in, or immediately under work existing before the current project.

13.2

The additional rules for work to existing buildings are to be read in conjunction with the preceding rules in the appropriate Work Sections.

13.3

A description of the additional Preliminaries/General conditions which are pertinent to the work to the existing building shall be given, drawing attention to any specific requirements due to the nature of the work.

14. General definitions

14.1

Where the rules require work to be described as curved with the radii stated details shall be given of the curved work including, if concave or convex, if conical or spherical, if to more than one radius and shall state the radius or radii.

14.2

The radius stated shall be the mean radius measured to the centre line of the material unless otherwise stated.

INFORMATION PROVIDED				MEASUREMENT RULES	DEFINITION RULES	COVERAGE RULES	SUPPLEMENTARY INFORMATION
P1 Location drawings as defined in General Rule 5.1							
P2 Information to facilitate visiting site and addresses where drawings or other information additional to that required by these rules or other listed information may be inspected							
CLASSIFICATION TABLE					D1 A fixed charge is for work the cost of which is to be considered as independent of duration	C1 Works of a temporary nature are deemed to include rates, fees and charges related thereto in Sections A36, A41, A42, and A44	
A10 Project particulars					D2 A time related charge is for work the cost of which is to be considered as dependent on duration		
1 Project particulars	1 Name, nature and location		item				
	2 Names and addresses of Employer and Consultants						
A11 Drawings							
1 Drawings	1 List of drawings from which the bills of quantities were prepared		item				
A12 The site/Existing buildings							
1 The site/Existing buildings	1 Site boundaries		item				
	2 Existing buildings on or adjacent to the site						
	3 Existing mains/services						
	4 Others, details stated						
A13 Description of the work							
1 Description of the work	1 Elements of each new building		item	M1 Given only when the equivalent information is not indicated on the drawings provided			
	2 Dimensions and shape relating to each building	1 Plan area and perimeter at each floor level					
		2 Heights between floors					
		3 Total height					
	3 Details of related work by others						

A20 The Contract/Sub-contract

1 Form of Contract
  1 Schedule of clause headings of standard conditions
  2 Special conditions or amendments to standard conditions
  3 Appendix insertions
  4 Employer's insurance responsibility
  5 Performance guarantee bond

	item	1 Under deed

A30 Employer's requirements: Tendering/Sub-letting/Supply

1 Employer's requirements or limitations
  1 Details stated

	1 Fixed charge	item
	2 Time related charge	

A31 Employer's requirements: Provision, content and use of documents

1 Employer's requirements or limitations
  1 Details stated

	1 Fixed charge	item
	2 Time related charge	

A32 Employer's requirements: Management of the works

1 Employer's requirements or limitations
  1 Details stated

	1 Fixed charge	item
	2 Time related charge	

A33 Employer's requirements: Quality standards/control

1 Employer's requirements or limitations
  1 Details stated

	1 Fixed charge	item
	2 Time related charge	

A34 Employer's requirements: Security/Safety/Protection

1 Employer's requirements or limitations, details stated
  1 Noise and pollution control
  2 Maintain adjoining buildings
  3 Maintain public and private roads
  4 Maintain live services
  5 Security
  6 Protection of work in all sections
  7 Others

	1 Fixed charge	item
	2 Time related charge	

CLASSIFICATION TABLE				MEASUREMENT RULES	DEFINITION RULES	COVERAGE RULES	SUPPLEMENTARY INFORMATION
A35 Employer's requirements: Specific limitations on method/sequence/timing							
1 Employer's requirements or limitations, details stated	1 Design constraints	1 Fixed charge	item				
	2 Method and sequence of work	2 Time related charge					
	3 Access						
	4 Use of the site						
	5 Use or disposal of materials found						
	6 Start of work						
	7 Working hours						
	8 Others						
A36 Employer's requirements: Facilities/Temporary work/Services							
1 Employer's requirements or limitations, details stated	1 Offices	1 Fixed charge	item				
	2 Sanitary accommodation	2 Time related charge					
	3 Temporary fences, hoardings, screens and roofs						
	4 Name boards						
	5 Technical and surveying equipment						
	6 Temperature and humidity						
	7 Telephone/Facsimile installation and rental/maintenance						
	8 Others						
	9 Telephone/Facsimile call charges		prov sum			C2 Heating, lighting, cleaning and maintenance are deemed to be included	
A37 Employer's requirements: Operation/Maintenance of the finished building							
1 Employer's requirements or limitations	1 Details stated	1 Fixed charge	item				
		2 Time related charge					

A40 Contractor's general cost items: Management and staff

1 Management and staff	1 Fixed charge 2 Time related charge	item		D3 Management and staff includes management, trades supervision, engineering, programming and production, quantity surveying support staff and the like	

A41 Contractor's general cost items: Site accommodation

1 Site accommodation	1 Fixed charge 2 Time related charge	item	1 Made available by the Employer, details and conditions stated	D4 Site accommodation includes offices, laboratories, cabins, stores, compounds, canteens, sanitary facilities and the like	C3 General attendance is deemed to include the use of the Contractor's temporary roads, pavings and paths, standing scaffolding, standing power operated hoisting plant, the provision of temporary lighting and water supplies, clearing away rubbish, provision of space for the sub-contractor's own offices and the storage of his plant and materials and the use of messrooms, sanitary accommodation and welfare facilities provided by the Contractor

A42 Contractor's general cost items: Services and facilities

1 Services and facilities 1 Power 2 Lighting 3 Fuels 4 Water 5 Telephone and administration 6 Safety, health and welfare 7 Storage of materials 8 Rubbish disposal 9 Cleaning 10 Drying out 11 Protection of work in all sections 12 Security 13 Maintain public and private roads 14 Small plant and tools 15 Others 16 General attendance on nominated sub-contractors	1 Fixed charge 2 Time related charge	item	1 Made available by the Employer, details and conditions stated	D5 Items listed are not exhaustive and are for convenience of pricing only

A Preliminaries/General conditions continued

CLASSIFICATION TABLE				MEASUREMENT RULES	DEFINITION RULES	COVERAGE RULES	SUPPLEMENTARY INFORMATION
A43 Contractor's general cost items: Mechanical plant							
1 Mechanical plant	1 Cranes 2 Hoists 3 Personnel transport 4 Transport 5 Earthmoving plant 6 Concrete plant 7 Piling plant 8 Paving and surfacing plant 9 Others.	item	1 Fixed charge 2 Time related charge	1 Made available by the Employer, details and conditions stated		D6 Items listed are not exhaustive and are for convenience of pricing only	
A44 Contractor's general cost items: Temporary works							
1 Temporary works	1 Temporary roads 2 Temporary walkways 3 Access scaffolding 4 Support scaffolding and propping 5 Hoardings, fans, fencing etc. 6 Hardstanding 7 Traffic regulations 8 Others	item	1 Fixed charge 2 Time related charge	1 Made available by the Employer, details and conditions stated		D7 Items listed are not exhaustive and are for convenience of pricing only	
A50 Work/Materials by the Employer							
1 Work/Materials by the Employer	1 Work by others directly employed by the Employer 2 Attendance on others directly employed by the Employer, details stated 3 Materials provided by or on behalf of the Employer, details stated	item					

A51 Nominated sub-contractors

1 Nominated sub-contractors	1 Sub-contractor's work	1 Description stated in accordance with General Rule 10.3	p c sum		
	2 Main contractor's profit		%		M2 General attendance on sub-contractor's work is measured in Section A42
	3 Special attendance, details stated	1 Scaffolding 2 Access roads 3 Hardstandings 4 Positioning 5 Storage 6 Power 7 Temperature and humidity 8 Others	item	1 Fixed charge 2 Time related charge	

D8 Scaffolding under this rule is special scaffolding, scaffolding additional to the Contractor's standing scaffolding, or standing scaffolding required to be altered or retained

D9 Positioning includes unloading, distributing, hoisting and placing in position giving in the case of significant items the weight and/or size and position relative to ground level or other datum

A52 Nominated suppliers

1 Nominated suppliers	1 Supplier's materials	1 Description stated	p c sum	M3 Fixing only such items is measured in the appropriate Work Section
	2 Main contractor's profit		%	

C1 Fixing only such items is deemed to include unloading, storing, hoisting the goods and materials and returning packaging materials to the nominated supplier

S1 Particulars of any costs to be paid of conveying goods and materials to the site and/or of any special packing or similar requirements

A53 Work by statutory authorities

1 Work by statutory authorities	1 Work by the local authority
	2 Work by statutory undertakings — prov sum

D10 Work by statutory authorities includes work by public companies responsible for statutory work when executing their statutory duty

A54 Provisional work

1 Provisional work	1 Defined
	2 Undefined — prov sum

D11 For defined and undefined provisional sums see General Rule 10

A55 Dayworks

1 Dayworks	1 Labour
	2 Materials
	3 Plant — prov sum

C Demolition/Alteration/Renovation

C10 Demolishing structures
C30 Shoring

INFORMATION PROVIDED

P1 The following information is shown either on location drawings under A Preliminaries/General conditions or on further drawings which accompany the bills of quantities:
(a) the location and extent of existing structures to be demolished

CLASSIFICATION TABLE

				MEASUREMENT RULES	DEFINITION RULES	COVERAGE RULES	SUPPLEMENTARY INFORMATION
				M1 The rules within this Section apply to works to existing buildings as defined in the General Rules			
1 Demolishing all structures 2 Demolishing individual structures 3 Demolishing parts of structures	1 Description sufficient for identification	1 Levels to which structures are demolished	item				
			1 Materials remaining the property of the Employer 2 Materials for re-use 3 Making good structures 4 Leaving parts of existing walls temporarily in position to act as buttresses 5 Temporarily diverting, maintaining or sealing off existing services 6 Toxic or other special waste	M2 Only temporarily diverting, maintaining or sealing off existing services is measured under this rule	D1 Materials arising from demolitions are deemed to be the property of the Contractor unless otherwise stated D2 Demolishing parts of structures excludes items covered by Section C20	C1 Demolition items are deemed to include: (a) disposal of materials other than those remaining the property of the Employer or those for re-use (b) temporary support incidental to demolitions which is at the discretion of the Contractor	S1 Method of demolition where by specific means S2 Setting materials remaining the property of the Employer or those for re-use S3 Employer's restrictions on methods of disposal of materials
4 Support of structures not to be demolished 5 Support of roads and the like	1 Position and type of shoring and nature of structure or road to be shored stated	1 Providing and erecting 2 Maintaining, duration stated 3 Adapting, details stated 4 Clearing away 5 Cutting holes in the structure, details stated 6 Making good all work disturbed	item		D3 Support is other than temporary support incidental to demolitions	C2 Support is deemed to include nails, wedges and bolts	

	1 Dimensioned description			item	
6 Temporary roofs				1 Providing and erecting	
7 Temporary screens				2 Maintaining, duration stated	
				3 Adapting, details stated	
				4 Clearing away	
				5 Disposing of rainwater, details stated	
				6 Providing openings, details stated	
					S4 Details of weather and dust proofing requirements

INFORMATION PROVIDED

P1 The following information is shown either on location drawings under · A Preliminaries/General conditions or on further drawings which accompany the bills of quantities:

(a) the scope and location of the work relative to the existing layout indicating the existing structure

CLASSIFICATION TABLE

First Division	Second Division	Third Division	Unit
1 Removing fittings and fixtures	1 Details sufficient for identification stated	1 Making good structures	item
2 Removing plumbing and engineering installations	2 Dimensioned description sufficient for identification including type and thickness of existing structure	2 Extending and making good finishings	
3 Removing finishings		3 Inserting new work, details stated	
4 Removing coverings		4 Toxic or other special waste	
5 Cutting openings or recesses			
6 Cutting back projections			
7 Cutting to reduce thickness			
8 Filling in openings			
9 Temporary roofs	1 Dimensioned description	1 Providing and erecting	item
10 Temporary screens		2 Maintaining, duration stated	
		3 Adapting, details stated	
		4 Clearing away	
		5 Disposing of rainwater, details stated	
		6 Providing openings, details stated	

MEASUREMENT RULES

M1 The rules within this Section apply to works to existing buildings as defined in the General Rules

M2 Any operation to existing buildings involving removal of existing materials (other than for bonding purposes or renewal) is measured within this Section

M3 Details stated for inserting new work are the equivalent of those details required by the rules for the measurement of the same in other work sections

DEFINITION RULES

D1 Materials arising from alterations - spot items are the property of the Contractor unless otherwise stated

D2 Location is stated relative to existing building

D3 Inserting new work includes re-fixing or re-using removed materials

COVERAGE RULES

C1 Shoring and scaffolding where by specific means and making good all work disturbed by such shoring and scaffolding is deemed to be included within each item

C2 Alterations - spot items are deemed to include:

(a) disposal of materials other than those remaining the property of the Employer or those for re-use

(b) work incidental to alterations - spot items which is at the discretion of the Contractor

(c) all new fixing or joining materials required

SUPPLEMENTARY INFORMATION

S1 Method of operation, where by specific means

S2 Setting aside and storing materials remaining the property of the Employer or those for re-use

S3 Employer's restrictions on methods of disposal of materials

S4 Employer's restrictions on methods of shoring and scaffolding to be used

S5 Details of weather and dust proofing requirements

INFORMATION PROVIDED

P1 The following information is shown either on location drawings under A Preliminaries/General conditions or on further drawings which accompany the bills of quantities:

(a) the scope and location of the work relative to the existing layout indicating the existing structure

CLASSIFICATION TABLE

				Unit
1 Cutting out defective concrete and replacing with new	1 Dimensioned description	1 Plain, details stated	1 Treatment of reinforcement, details stated	m²
		2 Reinforced, details stated	2 Anchored mesh reinforcement, details stated	m
		3 Gun applied, details stated		nr
2 Resin or cement impregnation/injection	1 Dimensioned description	1 Concrete, details stated	1 Centres of drilling holes	m²
		2 Brickwork, details stated	2 Removing existing finishes	m
		3 Blockwork, details stated		nr
		4 Stonework, details stated		
3 Cutting out decayed, defective or cracked work and replacing with new	1 Size and depth or thickness stated	1 Brickwork, details stated	1 Making good with materials other than to match existing, details stated	m²
		2 Blockwork, details stated		m
		3 Stonework, details stated		nr
4 Repointing	1 Size and depth of raking out of existing joint	1 Brickwork, details stated	1 Type of pointing	m²
		2 Blockwork, details stated		
		3 Stonework, details stated		

MEASUREMENT RULES

M1 The rules within this Section apply to works to existing buildings as defined in the General Rules

M2 Details stated include bond and size of component

DEFINITION RULES

D1 Materials arising are the property of the Contractor unless otherwise stated

D2 Locations stated relative to the existing building

COVERAGE RULES

C1 Shoring and scaffolding incidental to the work and making good all work disturbed by such shoring and storing materials remaining the property of the Employer or those for re-use

C2 Work to existing buildings items are deemed to include:
(a) disposal of materials other than those remaining the property of the Employer or those for re-use
(b) incidental work which is at the discretion of the Contractor
(c) all new fixing or joining materials required

C3 Formwork and making good to match existing are deemed to be included

C4 Work is deemed to include making good holes and finishes on completion

C5 Work is deemed to include making good to match existing

C6 Repointing is deemed to include making good to adjoining work

SUPPLEMENTARY INFORMATION

S1 Method of operation, where by specific means

S2 Setting aside and storing materials remaining the property of the Employer or those for re-use

S3 Employer's restrictions on methods of disposal of materials

S4 Restrictions on the method of shoring and scaffolding

S5 Method of bonding new to existing

S6 Method of bonding new to existing

S7 Composition and mix of mortar

CLASSIFICATION TABLE					MEASUREMENT RULES	DEFINITION RULES	COVERAGE RULES	SUPPLEMENTARY INFORMATION
5 Removing stains and the like (nr)	1 > 1.00 m² 2 ≤ 1.00 m²	1 Concrete 2 Brickwork 3 Blockwork 4 Stonework	m² nr	1 Facings 2 Efflorescence 3 Stains 4 Graffiti 5 Vegetation 6 Algae 7 Others, details stated	M3 Number of areas is only stated in the description when measured in m²			S8 Special cleaning materials
6 Cleaning surfaces	1 Concrete 2 Brickwork 3 Blockwork 4 Stonework	1 Facings	m²	1 Washing 2 Abrasive blasting 3 Chemical treatments 4 Others, details stated				S9 Cleaning materials
7 Inserting new wall ties	1 Size and type of tie	1 Brickwork 2 Blockwork 3 Stonework	nr	1 Surface finishes, details stated	M4 Inserting new wall ties is measured here only when executed without demolition			S10 Details of cutting away and making good
8 Re-dressing to new profile	1 Detailed description and size of new profile 2 Detailed description and length and size of new profile		m nr		M5 Work is measured linear where of a continuous nature			
9 Artificial weathering	1 Concrete 2 Brickwork 3 Blockwork 4 Stonework		m²	1 To match existing				

INFORMATION PROVIDED	MEASUREMENT RULES	DEFINITION RULES	COVERAGE RULES	SUPPLEMENTARY INFORMATION
P1 The following information is shown either on location drawings under A Preliminaries/General conditions or on further drawings which accompany the bills of quantities: (a) the scope and location of the work relative to the existing layout indicating the existing structure				

CLASSIFICATION TABLE

				MEASUREMENT RULES	DEFINITION RULES	COVERAGE RULES	SUPPLEMENTARY INFORMATION
1 Chemical damp proof courses	1 Brickwork 2 Blockwork 3 Stonework	1 Thickness of wall stated	m	1 Centres of drilling holes 2 Removing existing finishes		C1 Works are deemed to include: (a) disposal of materials (b) making good to holes and finishes after injection	S1 Method of operation, where by specific means S2 Damp proof chemicals

C50 Repairing/Renovating metal
C51 Repairing/Renovating timber
C52 Fungus/Beetle eradication

INFORMATION PROVIDED	MEASUREMENT RULES	DEFINITION RULES	COVERAGE RULES	SUPPLEMENTARY INFORMATION
P1 The following information is shown either on location drawings under A Preliminaries/General conditions or on further drawings which accompany the bills of quantities: (a) the scope and location of the work				

CLASSIFICATION TABLE

			MEASUREMENT RULES	DEFINITION RULES	COVERAGE RULES	SUPPLEMENTARY INFORMATION
1 Repairing metal 2 Repairing timber 3 Treating existing timber	1 Dimensioned description	m² m nr	M1 The dimensioned description or dimensioned diagram (in conjunction with the Information Provided) must clearly identify all work in exploration, preparation and execution together with the associated works required	D1 Repairing includes renovation or refurbishment		S1 Such information as is appropriate to the repair, renovation or refurbishment of the item S2 Such information as is appropriate to the treatment of timber to eradicate fungus attacks or beetle infestation

D Groundwork

D20 Excavating and filling
Q20 Hardcore/Granular/Cement bound bases/sub-bases to roads/pavings

INFORMATION PROVIDED

P1 The following information is shown either on location drawings under A Preliminaries/General conditions or on further drawings which accompany the bills of quantities or stated as assumed:

(a) the ground water level and the date when it was established, defined as the pre-contract water level
(b) the ground water level is to be re-established at the time each excavation is carried out and is defined as the post contract water level
(c) ground water levels subject to periodic changes due to tidal or similar effects are so described giving the mean high and low water levels
(d) details of trial pits or boreholes including their location
(e) features retained
(f) live over or underground services indicating location
(g) pile sizes and layout in accordance with Sections D30 – D32 where applicable

CLASSIFICATION TABLE

				MEASUREMENT RULES	DEFINITION RULES	COVERAGE RULES	SUPPLEMENTARY INFORMATION
1 Site preparation	1 Removing trees			M1 Tree girths are measured at a height of 1.00 m above ground			
	2 Removing tree stumps	1 Girth 600 mm – 1.50 m	nr	M2 Stump girths are measured at the top			
		2 Girth 1.50 – 3.00 m					
		3 Girth > 3.00 m, girth stated					
	3 Clearing site vegetation	4 Description sufficient for identification stated	m²		D1 Site vegetation is bushes, scrub, undergrowth, hedges and trees and tree stumps ≤ 600 mm girth	C1 This work is deemed to include: (a) grubbing up roots (b) disposal of materials (c) filling voids	S1 Filling material described
	4 Lifting turf for preservation	1 Method of preserving, details stated	m²				

29

2 Excavating

Classification	First subdivision	Second subdivision	Unit	Supplementary information	Measurement rules	Definition rules	Coverage rules	Supplementary information
2 Excavating	1 Topsoil for preservation	1 Average depth stated	m²	1 Commencing level stated where > 0.25 m below existing ground level	M3 The quantities given are the bulk before excavating and no allowance is made for subsequent variations to bulk or for extra space for working space or to accommodate earthwork support			
	2 To reduce levels	1 Maximum depth ≤ 0.25 m	m³		M4 Excavating for ground beams not between piles is measured under 2.5 & 6.∗.∗			
	3 Basements and the like	2 Maximum depth ≤ 1.00 m			M5 If the post contract water level differs from the pre-contract water level the measurements are revised accordingly			
	4 Pits (nr)	3 Maximum depth ≤ 2.00 m			M6 To be measured where precautions are specifically required			
	5 Trenches, width ≤ 0.30 m	4 and thereafter in 2.00 m stages						
	6 Trenches, width > 0.30 m							
	7 For pile caps and ground beams between piles							
	8 To bench sloping ground to receive filling							
3 Items extra over any types of excavating irrespective of depth	1 Excavating below ground water level		m³			D2 Retaining a service is a precaution which is specifically required		S2 Nature of special requirement
	2 Next existing services	1 Type of service stated	m			D3 Rock is any material which is of such size or position that it can only be removed by wedges, special plant or explosives		
	3 Around existing services crossing excavation		nr					
4 Breaking out existing materials	1 Rock	1 Extra over any types of excavating irrespective of depth	m³	.		D4 Backfilling with special materials occurs where selected or treated excavated materials or imported materials are used	C2 Additional earthwork support, disposal, backfilling, work below ground water level and breaking out are deemed to be included	S3 Details of backfilling with special materials
	2 Concrete							
	3 Reinforced concrete							
	4 Brickwork, blockwork or stonework							
	5 Coated macadam or asphalt							
5 Breaking out existing hard pavings, thickness stated			m²					
6 Working space allowance to excavations	1 Reduce levels, basements and the like		m²		M7 Working space is measured where the face of the excavation is < 600 mm from the face of formwork, rendering, tanking or protective walls			
	2 Pits				M8 The area measured is calculated by multiplying the girth of the formwork, rendering, tanking or protective walls by the depth of excavation below the commencing level of the excavation			
	3 Trenches							
	4 Pile caps and ground beams between piles							

CLASSIFICATION TABLE					MEASUREMENT RULES	DEFINITION RULES	COVERAGE RULES	SUPPLEMENTARY INFORMATION
7 Earthwork support	1 Maximum depth ≤ 1.00 m 2 Maximum depth ≤ 2.00 m 3 and thereafter in 2.00 m stages	1 Distance between opposing faces ≤ 2.00 m 2 Distance between opposing faces 2.00 – 4.00 m 3 Distance between opposing faces > 4.00 m	m²	1 Curved 2 Below ground water level 3 Unstable ground 4 Next to roadways 5 Next to existing buildings 6 Left in	M9 Earthwork support is measured the full depth to all faces of excavation whether or not required except to: (a) face ≤ 0.25 m high (b) sloping faces of excavations where the angle of inclination is ≤ 45° from the horizontal (c) faces of excavations which abut existing walls, piers, or other structures M10 Earthwork support below ground water level or in unstable ground is measured from the commencing level of the excavation to the full depth M11 Earthwork support below ground water level is only measured where a corresponding item is measured in accordance with 3.1.0.0 and is adjusted accordingly if the post contract water level is different	D5 Earthwork support is deemed to include everything to uphold the sides of excavation by means other than interlocking steel piling which is measured in Section D32 D6 Earthwork support next to roadways occurs where the horizontal distance from the edge of the roadway or footpath is < the depth of the excavated face below the roadway or footpath D7 Earthwork support next to existing buildings occurs where the horizontal distance from the face supported to the nearest part of the foundations of the building, is < the depth of the excavated face below the bottom of the foundations D8 Unstable ground is running silt, running sand, loose gravel and the like	C3 Curved earthwork support is deemed to include any extra costs of curved excavation	
8 Disposal	1 Surface water 2 Ground water		item		M12 An item for disposal of ground water is only measured where a corresponding item is measured in accordance with 3.1, and is adjusted accordingly if the post contract water level is different	D9 Surface water is water on the surface of site and the like		
	2 Ground water	1 Off site 2 On site						
	3 Excavated material	1 Specified locations, details stated 2 Specified handling, details stated	m³		M13 The quantity given for disposal is the bulk before excavating and no allowance is made for subsequent variations to bulk or for extra space to accommodate earthwork support		C4 Any type of excavated or broken out material is deemed to be included	

Item	Classification 1	Classification 2	Unit	Classification 3	Measurement / Definition / Coverage Rules	Supplementary Information
9 Filling to excavations 10 Filling to make up levels 11 Filling to external planters and the like, position stated	1 Average thickness ≤ 0.25 m 2 Average thickness > 0.25 m	1 Arising from the excavations 2 Obtained from on site spoil heaps 3 Topsoil 4 Obtained off site, type stated	m³	1 Selected, details stated 2 Treated, details stated 3 Topsoil 4 Specified handling, details stated	M14 Filling is measured as equal to the void filled M15 The average thickness measured for filling is that after compaction M16 The position of external planters and the like is only stated where not at ground level	S4 Kind and quality of materials S5 Method of filling and compacting in layers
12 Surface packing to filling	1 To vertical or battered faces		m²			
13 Surface treatments	1 Applying herbicides		m²			S6 Kind and quality of materials and rate of application
	2 Compacting	1 Ground 2 Filling 3 Bottoms of excavations		1 Blinding, material stated	M17 Surface treatments may alternatively be given in the description of any superficial item M18 Specific blinding beds are measured as filling 10.*.*.* M19 Concrete blinding beds are measured in Section E10	C5 Compacting is deemed to include levelling and grading to falls and slopes ≤ 15° from horizontal S7 Method of compacting S8 Kind and quality of materials
	3 Trimming	1 Sloping surfaces 2 Sides of cuttings 3 Sides of embankments		1 In rock 1 Battered 2 Vertical 3 In rock	M20 Trimming sloping surfaces is only measured where the slope is > 15° from horizontal D10 Work is only described as battered where the slope > 15° from horizontal	
	4 Trimming rock to produce fair or exposed face					
	5 Preparing subsoil for top soil					S9 Method of preparing

INFORMATION PROVIDED

P1 The following information is shown either on location drawings under A Preliminaries/General conditions or on further drawings which accompany the bills of quantities:
- (a) the general piling layout
- (b) the positions of different types of piles
- (c) the positions of the work within the site and of existing services
- (d) the relationship to adjacent buildings

P2 Soil description:
- (a) the nature of the ground is given in accordance with Section D20 Information Provided
- (b) where work is carried out near canals, rivers, etc. or tidal waters, the level of the ground in relation to the normal levels of the canal or river etc. or to the mean Spring levels of high and low tidal waters, is stated; flood levels are stated where applicable

P3 Commencing levels:
- (a) the levels from which the work is expected to begin and from which measurements have been taken are stated; irregular ground is so described

CLASSIFICATION TABLE

Item	Sub-classification	Unit	Supplementary
1 Bored piles 2 Driven shell piles	1 Nominal diameter stated		
	1 Total number, commencing surface stated	nr	1 Preliminary piles 2 Contiguous bored piles 3 Raking, inclination ratio stated
	2 Total concreted length	m	
	3 Total bored or driven length, maximum length stated	m	
3 Pre-boring driven piles	1 Maximum depth stated	m	
4 Backfilling empty bores	1 Type of backfill material stated	m	
5 Items extra over piling	1 Breaking through obstructions	h	
	2 Enlarging bases for bored piles 3 Enlarging bases for driven shell piles		
	1 Diameter of enlarged base stated	nr	

MEASUREMENT RULES

M1 Bored and driven lengths are measured along the axes of the piles from the commencing surface to the bottom of the piles where the piles are designed for the load to be carried on the concrete shafts of bored piles and to the bottom of the casings of driven piles

M2 Pre-boring is only measured where it is specifically required

M3 Breaking through obstructions is only measured where obstructions are encountered above the founding stratum of the pile

DEFINITION RULES

D1 Piles comprising a driven light gauge casing which is first filled with concrete and then withdrawn are classed as driven shell piles where the piles are designed for the load to be carried on the concrete

D2 Filling such piles is not classed as filling hollow piles in accordance with Section D31:8.1.*.*

COVERAGE RULES

C1 Total concrete length is deemed to include concrete placed in excess of the completed length

C2 Pre-boring is deemed to include grouting up voids between sides of piles and bores

C3 The work is deemed to include work below the specified bottom

SUPPLEMENTARY INFORMATION

S1 Kind and quality of materials and mix details
S2 Tests of materials
S3 Type of grout
S4 Details of compaction

Item			Unit		Measurement rules	Coverage / Specification rules
6 Permanent casings	1 Internal diameter stated	1 Length ≤ 13 m (nr) 2 Length > 13 m (nr)	m	1 Wall thickness of casing stated	M5 Permanent casings are measured from the commencing surface	C4 Permanent casings are deemed to include driving heads and shoes S5 Type of material and finish to external surface S6 Details of driving heads and shoes where not at the discretion of the Contractor
7 Cutting off tops of piles (nr)	1 Nominal diameter stated	1 Total length	m	1 Tops of permanent casings		C5 Cutting off tops of piles is deemed to include preparation and integration of reinforcement into pile cap or ground beam and disposal
8 Reinforcement to piles	1 Nominal size of bars stated 2 Nominal size of helical bars stated	1 Nominal diameter of piles stated	t			C6 Reinforcement to piles is deemed to include tying wire, spacers, links and binders which are at the discretion of the Contractor S7 Kind and quality of materials
9 Disposal	1 Excavated materials	1 Off site 2 On site	m³	1 Specified locations, details stated 2 Specified handling, details stated	M6 The volume of disposal of surplus excavated materials is calculated from the nominal cross-sectional size of piles and their lengths measured in accordance with 1 & 2.1.2.∗ The volume of enlarged bases is added to this calculation	
10 Delays	1 Rig standing		h		M7 Delays are only measured where specifically authorised	C7 Delays are deemed to include associated labour
11 Pile tests	1 Details stated		nr			S8 Timing and details of tests

INFORMATION PROVIDED

P1 The following information is shown either on location drawings under A Preliminaries/General conditions or on further drawings which accompany the bills of quantities:
(a) the general piling layout
(b) the positions of different types of piles
(c) the positions of the work within the site and of existing services
(d) the relationship to adjacent buildings

P2 Soil description:
(a) the nature of the ground is given in accordance with Section D20 Information Provided
(b) where work is carried out near canals, rivers, etc. or tidal waters, the level of the ground in relation to the normal levels of the canal or river etc. or to the mean Spring levels of high and low tidal waters, is stated; flood levels are stated where applicable

P3 Commencing levels
(a) the levels from which the work is expected to begin and from which measurements have been taken are stated; irregular ground is so described

CLASSIFICATION TABLE

First division	Second division	Third division	Unit	Fourth division
1 Reinforced piles 2 Prestressed piles 3 Reinforced sheet piles 4 Hollow section piles	1 Nominal cross-sectional size stated	1 Total number driven, specified length and commencing surface stated	nr	1 Preliminary piles 2 Raking, inclination stated
		2 Total driven depth	m	
5 Items extra over piling		1 Redriving piles	nr	
6 Pre-boring		1 Maximum depth stated	m	
7 Jetting		1 Plain	m	
		2 Reinforced, details stated	m	
8 Filling hollow piles with concrete		1 Total number	nr	
		2 Plain	m	
9 Pile extensions		1 Total number	nr	
		2 Extension length ≤ 3.00 m	m	
		3 Extension length > 3.00 m	m	

MEASUREMENT RULES

M1 The measurement for the total driven depth includes for driving extended piles

M2 The driven depth is measured from the commencing surface to the bottom of the pile toe along the axis of the pile

M3 Redriving piles is only measured where it is specifically required

M4 Pre-boring is only measured where it is specifically required

DEFINITION RULES

D1 The total driven depth is that specifically required by the designer

COVERAGE RULES

C1 Driving heads and shoes are deemed to be included

C2 Pre-boring is deemed to include grouting up voids between sides of piles and bores

C3 Preparing heads, to receive pile extensions is deemed to be included

SUPPLEMENTARY INFORMATION

S1 Kind and quality of materials

S2 Tests of materials

S3 Details of driving heads and shoes

S4 Type of grout

S5 Specification of concrete and reinforcement

First Division	Second Division	Third Division	Unit	Rules
10 Cutting off tops of piles (nr)	1 Total length		m	C4 Cutting off tops of piles is deemed to include preparation and integration of reinforcement into pile cap or ground beam and disposal
11 Disposal	1 Excavated material	1 Off site 2 On site	m³	1 Specified locations, details stated 2 Specified handling, details stated M5 The volume of disposal of surplus excavated materials is calculated from the nominal cross-sectional size of piles and their depths measured in accordance with 1 – 4.1.2.✻
12 Delays		1 Rig standing	h	M6 Delays are only measured where they are specifically authorised C5 Delays are deemed to include associated labour
13 Pile tests		1 Details stated	nr	S6 Timing and details of tests

INFORMATION PROVIDED

P1 The following information is shown either on location drawings under A Preliminaries/General conditions or on further drawings which accompany the bills of quantities:
- (a) the general piling layout
- (b) the positions of different types of piles
- (c) the positions of the work within the site and of existing services
- (d) the relationship to adjacent buildings

P2 Soil description:
- (a) the nature of the ground is given in accordance with Section D20 Information Provided
- (b) where work is carried out near canals, rivers, etc. or tidal waters, the levels of the ground in relation to the normal levels of the canal or river etc. or to the mean Spring levels of high and low tidal water is stated; flood levels are stated where applicable

P3 Commencing levels:
- (a) the levels from which the work is expected to begin and from which measurements have been taken are stated; irregular ground is so described

CLASSIFICATION TABLE

				MEASUREMENT RULES	DEFINITION RULES	COVERAGE RULES	SUPPLEMENTARY INFORMATION
1 Isolated piles	1 Mass per metre and cross-sectional size, or section reference stated	1 Total number driven specified length and commencing surface stated	nr	M1 The measurement of the total driven depths includes for driving extended piles	D1 The specified length is that specifically required by the designer	C1 The cost of extraction is deemed to be included with piles so described	S1 Kind and quality of materials
				1 Preliminary piles			S2 Tests of materials
				2 Raking, inclination ratio stated			
		2 Total driven depth	m	M2 The driven depth is measured from the commencing surface to the bottom of the pile toe along the axis of the pile			
				3 To be extracted			
2 Interlocking piles	1 Section modulus and cross-sectional size, or section reference stated	1 Total area of specified length ≤ 14.00 m	m²	M3 The following separate items are required for each group of interlocking piles:			
		2 Total area of specified length 14.00 – 24.00 m		(a) one or more items for the total area of the group of piles divided into the ranges of specified lengths given in 2.1.1–3.*			
		3 Total area of specified length > 24.00 m		(b) an item for the total driven area of the group of piles			
		4 Total driven area		M4 The areas of items for interlocking piles are calculated by multiplying the mean undeveloped horizontal lengths of the pile walls formed (including lengths occupied by special piles) by the depths measured in accordance with the definitions of driven			

First Division	Second Division	Third Division	Unit	Measurement Rules	Coverage Rules	Additional Description Rules
				depths in the case of items for the driven areas and by the lengths measured in accordance with the definition of lengths in the case of items for the specified areas of piles		
3 Items extra over interlocking piles	1 Corners 2 Junctions 3 Closures 4 Tapers	1 Type stated	m	M5 The length measured for items extra over is the total length		
4 Isolated pile extensions	1 Mass per metre and cross-sectional size, or section reference stated	1 Total number	nr	M6 Separate items are required for the length of pile extensions and for the number of pile extensions	C2 The cost of extraction is deemed to be included with piles so described	
5 Interlocking pile extensions	2 Section modulus and cross-sectional size, or section reference stated	2 Extension length ≤ 3.00 m 3 Extension length > 3.00 m	m		C3 Pile extensions are deemed to include the work necessary to attach the extension to the pile	
					1 Preliminary piles 2 Raking, inclination ratio stated 3 To be extracted 4 Using materials arising from cutting off surplus lengths of other piles	
6 Cutting off surplus from specified lengths	1 Mass per metre and cross-sectional size, or section reference stated	1 Isolated piles (nr)	m	M7 The length measured is the surplus length of each pile	C4 Cutting off surplus from specified lengths of piles is deemed to include provision and filling of working space and disposal	
	2 Section modulus and cross-sectional size, or section reference stated	2 Interlocking piles (nr)	m			
					1 Preliminary piles 2 Raking, inclination ratio stated	
7 Cutting interlocking piles to form holes	1 Dimensioned description		nr			
8 Delays	1 Rig standing	1 Isolated piles 2 Interlocking piles	h	M8 Delays are only measured where specifically authorised	C5 Delays are deemed to include associated labour	
9 Pile tests	1 Details stated		nr			S3 Timing and details of tests

INFORMATION PROVIDED

P1 The following information is shown either on location drawings under A Preliminaries/General conditions or on further drawings which accompany the bills of quantities:

(a) the arrangement of diaphragm walls and their relationship to surrounding buildings

(b) the depths, lengths and thicknesses of diaphragm walls

P2 Soil description:

(a) the nature of the ground is given in accordance with Section D20 Information Provided

(b) where work is carried out near canals, rivers, etc. or tidal waters, the level of the ground in relation to the normal level of the canal or river etc. or to the mean Spring levels of high and low tidal waters is stated; flood levels are stated where applicable

P3 Commencing levels:

(a) the levels from which the work is expected to begin and from which measurements have been taken are stated

(b) irregular ground is so described

CLASSIFICATION TABLE

				MEASUREMENT RULES	DEFINITION RULES	COVERAGE RULES	SUPPLEMENTARY INFORMATION
1 Excavation and disposal	1 Thickness of wall stated	1 Maximum depth stated	m³	M1 The volume of excavation and disposal is calculated using the nominal lengths and depths of the walls. The depths are taken from the commencing surface			S1 Details of support fluid S2 Limitations on method of disposal
2 Items extra over excavation	1 Breaking out existing materials	1 Rock 2 Concrete	m³				
	2 Breaking out existing hard pavings; thickness stated	3 Reinforced concrete 4 Brickwork, blockwork or stonework 5 Coated macadam or asphalt	m²				
3 Backfilling empty trench	1 Type of fill material stated		m³				
4 Concrete	1 Thickness of wall stated		m³	M2 Concrete volume is measured net except that deductions are not made for the following: (a) reinforcement (b) steel sections of area ≤ 0.50 m² (c) cast in accessories (d) voids ≤ 0.05 m³ in volume			S3 Materials and mix details S4 Tests

First Division	Second Division	Third Division	Unit	Measurement Rules	Coverage / Additional Description Rules
5 Reinforcement				M3 Reinforcement is measured in accordance with Section E30 and the mass measured includes that of stiffening, lifting and supporting steel cast in where specifically required	
6 Cutting off to specified level	1 Details stated		m		C1 Cutting off to specified level is deemed to include provision and filling of working space and disposal
7 Trimming and cleaning face of diaphragm wall	1 Thickness of wall stated		m²		
8 Waterproofed joints	1 Type and method stated		m	M4 Waterproofed joints are only measured where they are specifically required	
9 Guide walls	1 One side 2 Both sides		m	M5 The lengths measured for guide walls are those of the diaphragm walls	
10 Ancillary work in connection with diaphragm walling	1 Preparing cast in pockets or chases at junctions, details stated	1 Limitations on design and construction stated	item	M6 The extent to which excavation, disposal, support, concrete, reinforcement, formwork, and the like are to be included is stated in the item description	C2 Preparing cast in pockets or chases is deemed to include removing formwork and preparing cast in reinforcement
	2 Excavating temporary backfill		m³		
	3 Removal of guide walls	1 One side 2 Both sides	m	M7 The lengths measured for guide walls are those of the diaphragm walls	C3 Removal of guide walls is deemed to include disposal S5 Limitations on method of disposal
11 Delays	1 Rig standing		h	M8 Delays are only measured where they are specifically authorised	C4 Delays are deemed to include associated labour
12 Tests	1 Details stated		nr		S6 Timing and details of tests

INFORMATION PROVIDED

P1 The following information is shown either on location drawings under A Preliminaries/General conditions or on further drawings which accompany the bills of quantities:
  (a) the location and extent of the work
  (b) details of the existing structure to be underpinned

P2 Information regarding the nature of excavation work is described in accordance with Section D20 Information Provided

P3 The limit of length carried out in one operation and the number of sections the Contractor is permitted to undertake at one time

CLASSIFICATION TABLE

				MEASUREMENT RULES	DEFINITION RULES	COVERAGE RULES	SUPPLEMENTARY INFORMATION
1 Temporary support for existing structures	1 Particular requirements stated		item				S1 Details of making good
2 Excavating	1 Preliminary trenches 2 Underpinning pits	1 Maximum depth ≤ 0.25 m 2 Maximum depth ≤ 1.00 m 3 Maximum depth ≤ 2.00 m 4 and thereafter in 2.00 m stages	1 Curved 2 From one side only 3 From both sides	m³	M1 Width allowances are related to the total depth of excavation measured from the top of the preliminary trench to the base of the underpinning pit as follows: (a) 1 m where the total depth is ≤ 1.5 m (b) 1.5 m where the total depth is 1.5 – 3m (c) 2 m where the total depth is > 3 m M2 The width of a preliminary trench is calculated as the sum of any projection of the retained foundation beyond the face of the wall plus any projection of the underpinning beyond the face of the retained foundation plus the width allowance M3 The width of an underpinning pit is calculated as the sum of the width of retained foundation plus any projection of the underpinning beyond the face of the retained foundation plus the width allowance	D1 Preliminary trenches extend down to the underside of existing foundations D2 Underpinning pits extend from the underside of existing foundations down to the base of the underpinning excavation		
3 Items extra over any type of excavating irrespective of depth				M4 Items extra over are measured in accordance with Section D20:3–5.∗.∗.∗			

4 Earthwork support	1 Preliminary trenches 2 Underpinning pits			m²	M5 Earthwork support is measured in accordance with Section D20:7.*.*.* M6 Earthwork support to underpinning pits is measured to the back, front and both ends of the underpinning pits and also between each section of the underpinning
5 Cutting away existing projecting foundations	1 Masonry 2 Concrete	1 Maximum width and depth of projection stated		m	
6 Preparing the underside of the existing work to receive the pinning up of the new work	1 Width of existing work stated			m	
7 Disposal					M7 Disposal of water and excavated material are measured in accordance with Section D20:8.*.*.*
8 Filling					M8 Filling is measured in accordance with Section D20:9 & 10.*.*.*
9 Surface treatments					M9 Surface treatments are measured in accordance with Section D20:13.*.*.*
10 Concrete 11 Formwork 12 Reinforcement 13 Brickwork 14 Tanking					M10 Concrete, formwork, reinforcement, brickwork and tanking are measured in accordance with the appropriate Work Sections

E10 In situ concrete

INFORMATION PROVIDED

P1 The following information is shown either on location drawings under A Preliminaries/General conditions or on further drawings which accompany the bills of quantities:

(a) the relative positions of concrete members

(b) the size of members

(c) the thickness of slabs

(d) the permissible loads in relation to casting times

CLASSIFICATION TABLE

		m³	MEASUREMENT RULES	DEFINITION RULES	COVERAGE RULES	SUPPLEMENTARY INFORMATION
1 Foundations 2 Ground beams 3 Isolated foundations		1 Reinforced 2 Reinforced > 5% 3 Sloping ≤ 15° 4 Sloping > 15° 5 Poured on or against earth or unblinded hardcore	M1 Concrete volume is measured net except that deductions are not made for the following: (a) reinforcement (b) steel sections of area ≤ 0.50 m² (c) cast in accessories (d) voids ≤ 0.05 m³ in volume (except voids in troughed and coffered slabs) M2 The thickness range stated in descriptions excludes projections and recesses M3 The thickness range stated of coffered and troughed slabs is measured overall	D1 Foundations include attached column bases and attached pile caps D2 Isolated foundations include isolated column bases, isolated pile caps and machine bases D3 Beds include: (a) blinding beds (b) plinths (c) thickenings of beds D4 Slabs include: (a) attached beams and beam casings whose depth is ≤ three times their width (depth measured below the slab) (b) column drop heads D5 Coffered and troughed slabs include margins whose width is ≤ 500mm. Wider margins are included with ordinary slabs D6 Walls include attached columns and piers	C1 Concrete is deemed to include finishing as struck from basic finish formwork or with a non-mechanical tamped finish unless otherwise required under worked finishes	S1 Kind and quality of materials and mix details S2 Tests of materials and finished work S3 Measures to achieve watertightness S4 Limitations on method, sequence, speed or size of pouring S5 Methods of compaction and curing S6 Requirement for beds to be laid in bays
4 Beds	1 Thickness ≤ 150 mm 2 Thickness 150 – 450 mm 3 Thickness > 450 mm					
5 Slabs 6 Coffered and troughed slabs						
7 Walls 8 Filling hollow walls 9 Beams		1 Reinforced 2 Reinforced > 5%				
10 Beam casings	1 Isolated 2 Isolated deep 3 Attached deep					

		Unit		Measurement / Definition rules
11 Columns		m³		M4 Columns are only measured as such when isolated and when their length on plan is ≤ four times their thickness
12 Column casings				D7 Deep beams and beam casings are those whose depth (measured below the slab where attached) is > three times their width
13 Staircases				D8 Staircases include landings and strings
14 Upstands				D9 Upstands exclude kickers
15 Items extra over the in situ concrete in which they occur	1 Working around heating panels			D10 Monolithic finishes include those which are cast onto concrete by lining onto formwork
	2 Monolithic finishes, thickness stated	m²	1 Top surface sloping ≤ 15° 2 Top surface sloping > 15°	M5 The area measured is the system area
16 Grouting	1 Stanchion bases 2 Grillages	nr		
17 Filling	1 Mortices	nr		
	2 Holes, (nr)	m³		
	3 Chases > 0.01 m²	m³		
	4 Chases ≤ 0.01 m²	m		

44

INFORMATION PROVIDED

P1 The following information is shown either on location drawings under A Preliminaries/General conditions or on further drawings which accompany the bills of quantities:

(a) the relative positions of gun applied concrete members

(b) the permissible loads in relation to casting times

CLASSIFICATION TABLE

				MEASUREMENT RULES	DEFINITION RULES	COVERAGE RULES	SUPPLEMENTARY INFORMATION
1 Slabs	1 Thickness stated	1 Tops 2 Soffits	m² 1 Curved	M1 Reinforcement is measured in Section E30			S1 Kind and quality of materials S2 Preparatory work S3 Method of application and finish
2 Walls							
3 Beams							
4 Columns							

E20 Formwork for in situ concrete

INFORMATION PROVIDED

P1 The following information is shown either on location drawings under A Preliminaries/General conditions or on further drawings which accompany the bills of quantities:
(a) the relative positions of concrete members
(b) the size of members
(c) the thickness of slabs
(d) the permissible loads in relation to casting times

CLASSIFICATION TABLE

Classification	Sub-classification	Detail (unit)	Further detail
1 Sides of foundations 2 Sides of ground beams and edges of beds 3 Edges of suspended slabs 4 Sides of upstands 5 Steps in top surfaces 6 Steps in soffits 7 Machine bases and plinths	1 Plain vertical	1 Height > 1.00 m (m²)	1 Left in 2 Permanent
	2 Dimensioned description	1 Height ≤ 250 mm 2 Height 250 – 500 mm 3 Height 500 mm – 1.00 m (m)	
8 Soffits of slabs	1 Slab thickness ≤ 200 mm 2 and thereafter in 100 mm stages	1 Height to soffit ≤ 1.50 m 2 and thereafter in 1.50 m stages (m²)	1 Height in 2 Permanent
9 Soffits of landings (nr)		1 Horizontal 2 Sloping ≤ 15° 3 Sloping > 15°	3 Left in 4 Permanent
10 Soffits of coffered or troughed slabs	1 Size of mould and profile, centres of mould, and slab thickness stated		1 Left in 2 Permanent
11 Top formwork			

MEASUREMENT RULES

M1 Except where otherwise stated, formwork is measured to concrete surfaces of the finished structure which require temporary support during casting

M2 Curved work is so described with the radii stated

M3 Passings of ground beams are not deducted from area of formwork

M4 Voids ≤ 5.00 m² irrespective of location are not deducted from the area measured

M5 Soffits of coffered or troughed slabs are measured as if to a plain surface

M6 The thickness stated of the coffered or troughed slabs is measured overall

M7 Top formwork is measured for surfaces sloping > 15° or where otherwise specifically required

DEFINITION RULES

D1 Plain formwork surfaces are those which contain no steps, rebates, pockets or other discontinuities

D2 Formwork left in is that which is not designed to remain in position but is nonetheless impossible to remove

D3 Permanent formwork is that which is designed to remain in position

D4 Foundations include bases and pile caps

D5 Edges of suspended slabs exclude those associated with attached beams at slab perimeters

D6 Formwork to soffits of slabs includes formwork to landings occurring at floor levels

D7 Soffits of coffered or troughed slabs include margins which are ≤ 500 mm wide

COVERAGE RULES

C1 Formwork is deemed to include adaptation to accommodate projecting pipes, reinforcing bars and the like

C2 Formwork is deemed to include all cutting, splayed edges and the like

SUPPLEMENTARY INFORMATION

S1 Kind and quality of materials and propping requirements for permanent formwork

S2 Basic finish where not at the discretion of the Contractor

CLASSIFICATION TABLE					MEASUREMENT RULES	DEFINITION RULES	COVERAGE RULES	SUPPLEMENTARY INFORMATION
12 Walls	1 Vertical 2 Battered	m²	1 Height > 3.00 m above floor level 2 Interrupted 3 To one side only, wall thickness and background to other side stated 4 Left in 5 Permanent to both sides 6 Permanent to one side only, wall thickness and background to other side stated		M8 Voids ≤ 5.00 m² irrespective of location are not deducted from the area measured for walls M9 The area measured for walls whose height is > 3.00 m includes the area below 3.00 m high M10 The area of wall kickers is not deducted	D8 Walls include isolated columns and column casings whose length on plan is > four times their thickness		
13 Beams (nr) 14 Beam casings (nr) 15 Columns (nr) 16 Column casings (nr)	1 Attached to slabs 2 Attached to walls 3 Isolated	m²	1 Regular shaped, shape stated 2 Irregular shaped, dimensioned diagram	m	1 Height to soffit ≤ 1.50 m 2 and thereafter in 1.50 m stages 3 Left in 4 Permanent	M11 Passings of subsidiary beams or other projections are not deducted from areas of formwork but such intersections are deemed to constitute the commencement of an additional member M12 Formwork to edges of suspended slabs associated with attached beams at slab perimeters is included with the measurement of the formwork to such beams M13 Recesses, nibs or rebates which occur in beam or column formwork measured in accordance with 13 – 16.*.2.* are included in the measurement of such formwork	D9 Where a downstand beam is formed by temporary formwork but the slab is supported by permanent formwork the downstand beam is regarded as an isolated beam D10 Regular shaped includes rectangular, circular, hexagonal or other definable regular shape	C3 Formwork to beams, columns and casings is deemed to include ends	
17 Recesses (nr) 18 Nibs (nr) 19 Rebates (nr)	1 Dimensioned description	m	1 Extra over the formwork in which they occur 2 Left in 3 Permanent			M14 Recesses, nibs and rebates are only measured as extra over on superficial items of formwork		C4 Formwork to recesses is deemed to include ends	
20 Extra over a basic finish for formed finishes		m²	1 Slabs 2 Walls 3 Beams 4 Columns 5 Others, stated			D11 Formed finishes are those where a finish other than a basic finish is required		S3 Details of formed finishes

First division	Second division	Third division	Unit		Measurement / Definition / Coverage / Supplementary rules
21 Wall kickers					M15 Formwork to wall kickers is measured along the centre line of the wall and is deemed to include both sides
22 Suspended wall kickers					
23 Wall ends, soffits and steps in walls	1 Plain	1 Width > 1.00 m	m	1 Left in	
24 Openings in walls		2 Width ≤ 250 mm	m²	2 Permanent	
	2 Dimensioned description	3 Width 250 – 500 mm	m		
		4 Width 500 mm – 1.00 m	m		
25 Stairflights (nr)	1 Width of stairflight stated, waist and risers described	1 String, width stated	m	1 Left in	M16 Lengths of stairflights are measured between top and bottom nosings
	2 Dimensioned diagram	2 String, dimensioned diagram		2 Permanent	M17 Widths are measured overall
		3 Junction with wall			C5 Formwork to stairflights is deemed to include soffits, risers and strings
					S4 Height where specifically required
26 Mortices	1 Girth ≤ 500 mm	1 Depth ≤ 250 mm	nr	1 Rectangular	D12 Mortices include pockets
27 Holes	2 Girth 500 mm – 1.00 m	2 Depth 250 – 500 mm	nr	2 Circular	D13 Holes are those ≤ 5.00 m²
	3 and thereafter in 1.00 m stages	3 Depth 500 mm – 1.00 m	nr	3 Irregular shape, dimensioned description	
		4 Depth > 1.00 m depth stated		4 Left in	
				5 Permanent	
28 Complex shapes	1 Dimensioned description			1 Left in	
	2 Dimensioned diagram			2 Permanent	

INFORMATION PROVIDED

P1 The following information is shown either on location drawings under A Preliminaries/General conditions or on further drawings which accompany the bills of quantities:

(a) the relative positions of concrete members
(b) the size of members
(c) the thickness of slabs
(d) the permissible loads in relation to casting times

CLASSIFICATION TABLE

				MEASUREMENT RULES	DEFINITION RULES	COVERAGE RULES	SUPPLEMENTARY INFORMATION
1 Bar	1 Nominal size stated	1 Straight 2 Bent 3 Curved	t	1 Horizontal, length 12.00 – 15.00 m 2 and thereafter in 3.00 m stages 3 Vertical, length 6.00 – 9.00 m 4 and thereafter in 3.00 m stages	M1 The weight of bar reinforcement excludes surface treatments and rolling margin M2 The stage lengths in the fourth column are the lengths before bending	D1 Horizontal bars include bars sloping ≤ 30° from horizontal D2 Vertical bars include bars sloping > 30° from horizontal	C1 Bar reinforcement is deemed to include hooks and tying wire, and spacers and chairs which are at the discretion of the Contractor	S1 Kind and quality of materials S2 Details of tests S3 Bending restrictions
		4 Links	nr					
2 Spacers and chairs	1 Dimensioned description			M3 Spacers, chairs and special joints are measured only where they are not at the discretion of the Contractor			
3 Special joint	2 Nominal size and type stated			M4 The area measured for fabric excludes laps.			
4 Fabric	1 Mesh reference and weight per m² stated		m²			C2 Fabric reinforcement is deemed to include laps, tying wire, all cutting and bending, and spacers and chairs which are at the discretion of the Contractor	S4 Minimum laps
		1 Bent 2 Strips in one width, width stated		M5 Voids ≤ 1.00 m² in area are not deducted		C3 Bent fabric reinforcement is deemed to include that wrapped around steel members	

INFORMATION PROVIDED	MEASUREMENT RULES	DEFINITION RULES	COVERAGE RULES	SUPPLEMENTARY INFORMATION
P1 The following information is shown either on location drawings under A Preliminaries/General conditions or on further drawings which accompany the bills of quantities:				
(a) the relative positions of concrete members				
(b) the size of members				
(c) the thickness of slabs				
(d) the permissible loads in relation to casting times				

CLASSIFICATION TABLE

			MEASUREMENT RULES			SUPPLEMENTARY INFORMATION
1 Members tensioned (nr)	1 Dimensioned description	nr	1 Composite construction	M1 Post tensioning is measured by the number of tendons in identical members		S1 Number, length, material and size of wires in tendons
						S2 Ducts, vents and grouting
						S3 Anchorages and end treatment
						S4 Stressing sequence, transfer stress, initial stress
						S5 Limitation on propping

INFORMATION PROVIDED	MEASUREMENT RULES	DEFINITION RULES	COVERAGE RULES	SUPPLEMENTARY INFORMATION
P1 Information is shown on location drawings under A Preliminaries/General conditions				

CLASSIFICATION TABLE

					MEASUREMENT RULES	DEFINITION RULES	COVERAGE RULES	SUPPLEMENTARY INFORMATION
1 Plain	1 Width or depth ≤ 150 mm	1 Dimensioned description	m	1 Curved	M1 Construction joints located at the discretion of the Contractor are not measured			S1 Kind and quality of materials
2 Formed	2 and thereafter in 150 mm stages				M2 The width or depth of joints is measured overall	D1 Plain joints are those which do not require formwork	C1 Formed joints are deemed to include formwork	S2 Details of fillers, waterstops, dowels, backing strips and reinforcement crossing joints
3 Cut								S3 Method of application
4 Sealants							C2 Work is deemed to include preparation, cleaners, primers and sealers	S4 Preparation of contact surfaces, cleaners, primers and sealers
5 Angles in waterstops			nr		M3 Angles and intersections are measured only where they are welded or purpose made			
6 Intersections in waterstops								

INFORMATION PROVIDED				MEASUREMENT RULES	DEFINITION RULES	COVERAGE RULES	SUPPLEMENTARY INFORMATION
P1 Information is shown on location drawings under A Preliminaries/General conditions				M1 Curved work is so described			S1 Description of finish required and method of achieving where not at the discretion of the Contractor
CLASSIFICATION TABLE							
1 Tamping by mechanical means 2 Power floating 3 Trowelling 4 Hacking 5 Grinding 6 Sandblasting 7 Finishings achieved by other means	m²	1 Sloping 2 Falls 3 Crossfalls 4 Soffits					
8 Cutting chases 9 Cutting rebates	1 Depth ≤ 50 mm 2 Depth 50 – 100 mm 3 Depth 100 – 150 mm 4 Depth > 150 mm, depth stated	m	1 Specific width stated 2 Making good 3 In reinforced concrete	M2 Width is required to be stated only where there is a specific width requirement			
10 Cutting mortices 11 Cutting holes	1 Depth ≤ 100 mm 2 Depth 100 – 200 mm 3 Depth 200 – 300 mm 4 Depth > 300 mm, depth stated	nr	1 Specific cross sectional size stated 2 Making good 3 In reinforced concrete	M3 Cross sectional size is required to be stated only where there is a specific cross sectional size requirement			

INFORMATION PROVIDED

P1 The following information is shown either on location drawings under A Preliminaries/General conditions or on further drawings which accompany the bills of quantities:

(a) the relative positions of concrete members

(b) the size of members

(c) the thickness of slabs

(d) the permissible loads in relation to casting times

CLASSIFICATION TABLE

				MEASUREMENT RULES	DEFINITION RULES	COVERAGE RULES	SUPPLEMENTARY INFORMATION
1 Type or name stated	1 Dimensioned description	1 Spacing dimensions stated	m² m nr	M1 Cast-in accessories are normally measured by number (nr). Linear or area measure may be used provided that any appropriate spacing dimensions are given in descriptions	D1 Cast-in accessories include anchor bolts, anchor boxes, anchor fixing bolts etc, dowels, column guards and isolated glass lenses. Cast-in accessories exclude reinforcement, tying wire, distance blocks, spacers, chairs, structural steelwork, hollow blocks, filler blocks, permanent formwork, joints and all components around which concrete is cast, but which are not fixed by the Contractor		S1 Kind and quality of materials and sizes or manufacturer's reference

E50 Precast concrete large units
F31 Precast concrete sills/lintels/copings/features
H40 Glass reinforced cement cladding/features
H50 Precast concrete slab cladding/features
K33 Concrete/Terrazzo partitions

INFORMATION PROVIDED

P1 The following information is either shown on location drawings under A Preliminaries/General conditions or on further drawings which accompany the bills of quantities:

(a) details of precast concrete members showing stressing arrangements
(b) full details of anchorages, ducts, sheathing and vents
(c) the relative positions of concrete members
(d) the size of members
(e) the thickness of slabs
(f) the permissible loads

CLASSIFICATION TABLE

Classification			Unit	MEASUREMENT RULES	DEFINITION RULES	COVERAGE RULES	SUPPLEMENTARY INFORMATION
1 Type or name stated	1 Dimensioned description	1 Reinforcement, details stated	nr	M1 Precast units are normally measured by number (nr). Linear measurement may be used where the length of units is at the discretion of the Contractor, where the individual units are of an identical standard length, or where otherwise identical units vary in their length. In these cases the number of units is stated		C1 Precast units are deemed to include moulds, materials, bedding, reinforcement, fixings, temporary supports, cast-in accessories and pretensioning	S1 Kind and quality of materials and mix details
	2 Dimensioned description (nr)	2 Cast-in accessories, details stated	m	M2 Where floor units are of the same length they may be measured in square metres and grouped together stating length			S2 Tests of materials and finished work
	3 Dimensioned description	1 Floor units, length stated	m²	M3 Where units are measured linear, angles, fair ends, stoolings and the like are enumerated as extra over the units			S3 Methods of compaction and curing
2 Items extra over the units on which they occur	1 Angles						S4 Bedding and fixing
	2 Fair ends						S5 Surface finishes
	3 Stoolings						S6 Kind and quality of pretensioning materials, spacing and stresses
	4 Others, details stated		nr				
3 Joints	1 Dimensioned profile description	1 Sizes of filling and sealants stated	m	M4 Enumerated joints may be given in the description of the precast items in which they occur			S7 Kind and quality of materials
	2 Dimensioned description		nr				

E60 Precast/Composite concrete decking

INFORMATION PROVIDED

P1 The following information is shown either on location drawings under A Preliminaries/General conditions or on further drawings which accompany the bill of quantities:

(a) details of purpose-made, prestressed concrete members showing stressing arrangements

(b) full details of anchorages, ducts, sheathing and vents

(c) the relative positions of concrete members

(d) the size of members

(e) the thickness of slabs

(f) the permissible loads

CLASSIFICATION TABLE

					MEASUREMENT RULES	DEFINITION RULES	COVERAGE RULES	SUPPLEMENTARY INFORMATION
1 Composite slabs	1 Thickness stated		1 Sloping ≤ 15°	m²	M1 The thickness stated for composite slabs is measured overall	D1 Composite slabs include margins ≤ 500 mm wide, wider margins are included with ordinary slabs	C1 Composite slabs are deemed to include solid concrete work and filling ends	S1 Kind and quality of materials, sizes and spacings of planks and blocks
			2 Sloping > 15°		M2 Composite slabs are measured over margins ≤ 500 mm wide			S2 Top finish
					M3 Margins > 500 mm wide are measured as ordinary slabs in Sections E10, E20 and E30			S3 Soffit finish
								S4 Margins
2 Formwork					M4 Formwork to in situ component of work is measured in accordance with Section E20			S5 Formwork
3 Reinforcement					M5 Reinforcement to in situ component of work is measured in accordance with Section E30			S6 Reinforcement and prestressing arrangements

F Masonry

F10 Brick/Block walling
F11 Glass block walling

INFORMATION PROVIDED

P1 The following information is shown either on location drawings under A Preliminaries/General conditions or on further drawings which accompany the bills of quantities:

(a) Plans of each floor level and principal sections showing the position of and the materials used in the walls

(b) External elevations showing the materials used

CLASSIFICATION TABLE

				MEASUREMENT RULES	DEFINITION RULES	COVERAGE RULES	SUPPLEMENTARY INFORMATION
1 Walls	1 Thickness stated	1 Vertical	m²	M1 Brickwork and blockwork unless otherwise stated are measured on the centre line of the material	D1 Thickness stated is nominal thickness unless defined otherwise below	C1 Brickwork and blockwork are deemed to include:	S1 Kind, quality and size of bricks or blocks
2 Isolated piers	2 Facework one side, thickness stated	2 Battering		M2 No deductions are made for the following:	D2 Facework is any work in bricks or blocks finished fair	(a) extra materials for curved work	S2 Type of bond
3 Isolated casings	3 Facework both sides, thickness stated	3 Tapering, one side		(a) voids ≤ 0.10 m²	D3 Work is deemed vertical unless otherwise described	(b) all rough and fair cutting	S3 Composition and mix of mortar
4 Chimney stacks	4 Tapering, both sides	4 Tapering, both sides		(b) flues, lined flues and flue blocks where voids and work displaced are together ≤ 0.25 m²	D4 Walls include skins of hollow walls	(c) forming rough and fair grooves, throats, mortices, chases, rebates and holes, stops and mitres	S4 Type of pointing
		1 Building against other work		M3 Deductions for string courses, lintels, sills, plates and the like are measured as regards height to the extent only of full brick or block courses displaced and as regards depth to the extent only of full half brick beds displaced	D5 Battering walls are sloping walls with parallel sides	(d) raking out joints to form a key	S5 Method of cutting where not at the discretion of the Contractor
		2 Bonding to other work		M4 Curved work is so described with the radii stated	D6 Tapering walls are walls of diminishing thickness	(e) labours in eaves filling	
		3 Used as formwork, details of temporary strutting stated		M5 Building against other work and bonding to other work is measured where the other work is existing or consists of a differing material	D7 Thickness stated for tapering walls is mean thickness	(f) labours in returns, ends and angles	
		4 Building overhand			D8 Isolated piers are isolated walls whose length on plan is ≤ four times their thickness, except where caused by openings	(g) centering	
						C2 Brickwork and blockwork bonded to another material is deemed to include extra material for bonding	

Classification	First division	Second division	Unit	Third division / Notes	Rules
5 Projections	1 Width and depth of projection stated	1 Vertical 2 Raking 3 Horizontal	m		D9 Projections are attached piers (whose length on plan is ≤ four times their thickness), plinths, oversailing courses and the like
6 Arches (nr)	1 Height on face, thickness and width of exposed soffit and shape of arch stated		m		M6 Arches are measured the mean girth or length on face
7 Isolated chimney shafts and the like (nr)	1 Size on plan, shape and overall height stated		m²	1 Building from outside scaffolding	
8 Boiler seatings	1 Thickness stated		m²		
9 Flue linings	1 Thickness stated		m		M7 Non brick masonry flue linings are measured in Section F30:11.1.0.0
10 Boiler seating kerbs	1 Shape and size stated		m		
11 Items extra over the work in which they occur	1 Specials, dimensioned description	1 Reveals 2 Angles 3 Intersections	m		
12 Closing cavities	1 Width of cavity and method of closing stated	1 Vertical 2 Raking 3 Horizontal	m		
13 Facework ornamental bands and the like, type stated	1 Flush 2 Sunk, depth of set back stated 3 Projecting, depth of set forward stated	1 Vertical, width stated 2 Raking, width stated 3 Horizontal, width stated 4 Others, details stated	m	1 Extra over the work in which they occur 2 Entirely of stretchers 3 Entirely of headers 4 Building overhand	D10 Radii stated are mean radii on face D11 Facework ornamental bands and the like are brick-on-edge bands, brick-on-end bands, basket pattern bands, moulded or splayed plinth cappings, moulded string courses, moulded cornices and the like
14 Facework quoins	1 Flush 2 Sunk, depth of set back stated 3 Projecting, depth of set forward stated	1 Mean girth stated	m	1 Extra over the work in which they occur 2 Cut and rubbed 3 Rusticated 4 Tile inserts included 5 Building overhand	M8 Facework quoins are measured on the vertical angle D12 Facework quoins are formed with facing bricks which differ in kind or size from the general facings S6 Method of jointing quoins to brick or blockwork

CLASSIFICATION TABLE				MEASUREMENT RULES	DEFINITION RULES	COVERAGE RULES	SUPPLEMENTARY INFORMATION
15 Facework sills	1 Dimensioned description	1 Vertical 2 Raking 3 Horizontal 4 Others, details stated	m	1 Extra over the work in which they occur 2 Building overhand 3 Set weathering			S7 Method of forming sills, thresholds, copings and steps
16 Facework thresholds							
17 Facework copings							
18 Facework steps							
19 Facework tumblings to buttresses		1 Extra over the work in which they occur	nr				
20 Facework key blocks							
21 Facework corbels							
22 Facework bases to pilasters							
23 Facework cappings to pilasters							
24 Facework cappings to isolated piers							
25 Bonding to existing	1 Thickness of new work stated		m				
26 Surface treatments	1 Type and purpose stated	1 Type of wall stated	m²		D13 This item does not include application of materials to the wall		

F20 Natural stone rubble walling
F21 Natural stone ashlar walling/dressings
F22 Cast stone walling/dressings

INFORMATION PROVIDED	MEASUREMENT RULES	DEFINITION RULES	COVERAGE RULES	SUPPLEMENTARY INFORMATION
P1 The following information is shown either on location drawings under A Preliminaries/General conditions or on further drawings which accompany the bills of quantities: (a) plans of each floor level and principal sections showing the position of and the materials used in the walls (b) external elevations showing the materials used	M1 Stonework is measured according to mean dimensions M2 No deduction is made for: (a) voids ≤ 0.10 m² (b) flues, lined flues and flue blocks where voids and work displaced are together ≤ 0.25 m² M3 Linear and enumerated items shall identify grooves, throats, flutes, rebates, cutting and mortices M4 Curved work is so described with the radii stated	D1 The thickness stated is the nominal thickness except where defined otherwise below D2 Stone dressings are those in walls of other materials D3 Dimensioned diagrams are given unless a written description is sufficient for full clarity D4 Work is deemed vertical unless otherwise described	C1 The work is deemed to include: (a) extra stone for joints (b) extra materials for curved work (c) mortices, (other than linear items) holes, stops and arrises (d) raking out joints to form key (e) metal cramps, slate dowels, metal dowels, lead plugs and the like (f) labours in returns, ends and angles (g) labours in eaves filling (h) dressed margins to rubble work (i) levelling uncoursed work (j) templets and patterns (k) rough and fair square cutting	S1 Kind and quality of materials and, for rubble walling, whether of random or squared stones, built with or without mortar and where coursed the average height of the courses or maximum and minimum heights of diminishing course S2 Coatings to backs of stones S3 Coatings to surface of finished work S4 Cleaning on completion S5 Composition and mix of mortar S6 Type of pointing S7 Method of jointing together and fixing S8 Thickness, mix and colour of the facing material to cast stonework S9 Stones not set on their natural bed S10 Type and positioning of metal cramps, slates, dowels, metal dowels, lead plugs and the like

CLASSIFICATION TABLE

			Unit
1 Walls 2 Chimney stacks	1 Thickness stated	1 Vertical 2 Battering 3 Tapering, one side 4 Tapering, both sides	m²
3 Isolated columns 4 Attached columns	1 Dimensioned description		m
5 Vaulting	1 Thickness and type stated		m²
6 Lintels 7 Sills 8 Mullions 9 Transoms	1 Dimensioned description 2 Dimensioned diagram		m
10 Quoin stones 11 Jamb stones	1 Attached 2 Attached with different finish, type of finish stated 3 Isolated		m
12 Slab architraves 13 Slab surrounds to openings	1 Dimensioned description		m

Enumerated descriptions:

1 Blocks > 1.50 m long
2 Blocks > 0.50 m³
3 Stone dressings
4 Faced one side
5 Faced both sides
6 Building against other work
7 Building against other work
8 Bonding to other work
9 Sunk to entasis; greatest size stated
10 Plain
11 Sunk
12 Circular
13 Circular-circular
14 Rusticated or fluted
15 Used as formwork, details of temporary strutting stated
16 With stoolings (nr)
17 Band courses with returned ends (nr)
18 Building overhand

MEASUREMENT RULES

M5 Building against other work and bonding to other work is measured where the other work is existing or consists of a differing material

M6 Quoins and jambs are measured on the vertical angle

DEFINITION RULES

D5 Battering walls are sloping walls with parallel sides

D6 Tapering walls are walls of diminishing thickness

D7 Thickness stated for tapering walls is mean thickness

D8 Walls include skins of hollow walls

D9 Columns are walls whose length on plan is ≤ four times their thickness, except where caused by openings

D10 Attached columns include attached piers and pilasters

D11 The dimensioned description stated for attached columns refers to the projection only

D12 Attached stones are those attached to the same type of stone walling

D13 Isolated stones are those attached to another form of construction

D14 Slabs are those which are not bonded to their surrounding work

COVERAGE RULES

C2 Battering and tapering walls are deemed to include the extra materials required

C3 Work is deemed to include extra material for bonding

SUPPLEMENTARY INFORMATION

S11 Method of bonding to backing

S12 Type and spacing of fixing and method of securing to backing

Item			Unit	Rules
14 Bands and the like, type stated		1 Vertical	m	M7 Mouldings are only measured separately on superficial items of masonry and attached piers. Mouldings are given in the description of linear items
15 Corbel courses		2 Raking		D15 Band courses and the like include mouldings, enrichments, cornices and the like
16 Copings		3 Horizontal		D16 Plain bands > 300 mm wide are measured as walling or facework
17 Handrails		4 Others, details stated		
18 Cappings				
19 Kerbs				
20 Cover stones				
21 Steps (nr)		1 Plain	m	
		2 Spandrel		D17 Spandrel steps are steps with sloping soffits
22 Winders		1 Stones (nr)	nr / m	
23 Landings				
24 Arches (nr)	1 Height of face, width of soffit and shape of arch stated		nr	M8 Arches are measured the mean girth or length on face
				M9 The quantity (nr) is only stated in an item which is measured linearly
25 Closing cavities	1 Width of cavity and method of closing stated	1 Vertical	m	
		2 Raking		
		3 Horizontal		
26 Rough raking or circular cutting	1 Thickness stated		m	
27 Fair raking or circular cutting				
28 Grooves	1 Size stated		m	M10 Grooves, throats, flutes, and rebates are only measured separately on superficial items of masonry and attached piers
29 Throats				
30 Flutes				
31 Rebates				
32 Chases	1 Rough	1 Girth ≤ 150 mm	m	
	2 Fair	2 and thereafter in 150 mm stages		

CLASSIFICATION TABLE			nr	MEASUREMENT RULES	DEFINITION RULES	COVERAGE RULES	SUPPLEMENTARY INFORMATION
33 Special purpose stones	1 Function stated	1 Plain cuboid, dimensions stated 2 Dimensioned description	nr	M11 Descriptions of stones are given as the smallest block from which each item can be obtained having regard in the case of natural stone to the plane in which the stone is required to be laid with relation to its quarry bed. The dimensions are taken over one mortar bed and one mortar joint			
34 Carvings 35 Sculptures	1 Character of work stated	1 Component drawing	nr	1 Providing models		C4 Carvings and sculptures are deemed to include: (a) selecting blocks of stone for size and quality (b) boasting for carving (c) working mouldings or similar members	
36 Centering	1 Arches 2 Tracery 3 Projecting masonry 4 Vaulting	1 Dimensioned description	nr	1 Sloping soffits 2 Maximum support height 3.00 – 4.50 m 3 and thereafter in 1.50 m stages 4 Left in	M12 A dimensioned description of centering gives the shape and width of the surface to be supported, the span of the soffit, and, in the case of arches, whether segmental, semicircular, invert and the like, stating the rise	C5 Centering is deemed to include: (a) strutting, shoring, bolting, wedging, easing, striking and removing (b) cutting (c) scribed and splayed edges (d) notching for key blocks, projecting voussoirs and the like	S13 Nature of supported surface

INFORMATION PROVIDED

P1 The following information is shown either on location drawings under A Preliminaries/General conditions or on further drawings which accompany the bills of quantities:
(a) plans of each floor level and principal sections showing the position of and the materials used in the walls
(b) external elevations showing the materials used

CLASSIFICATION TABLE

				Unit	MEASUREMENT RULES	DEFINITION RULES	COVERAGE RULES	SUPPLEMENTARY INFORMATION
					M1 Curved work is so described		C1 Accessories are deemed to include: (a) rough and fair cutting on walls around accessories (b) bedding and pointing accessories (c) extra materials for curved work	S1 Kind and quality of materials
1 Forming cavities	1 In hollow walls	1 Width of cavity stated	1 Rigid sheet cavity insulation, thickness stated	m²				S2 Type, size and spacing of wall ties S3 Type, thickness and method of fixing cavity insulation
	2 Between walls and other work							
2 Damp proof courses	1 Width ≤ 225 mm 2 Width > 225 mm	1 Vertical 2 Raking 3 Horizontal 4 Stepped	1 Cavity trays	m²	M2 No allowance is made for laps M3 No deduction is made for voids ≤ 0.50 m²		C2 Damp proof courses are deemed to include pointing exposed edges	S4 Gauge, thickness or substance of sheet materials S5 Number of layers S6 Composition and mix of bedding materials
3 Joint reinforcement	1 Width stated			m	M4 No allowance is made for laps			S7 Minimum laps
4 Weather fillets	1 Size stated			m			C3 Fillets are deemed to include ends and angles	
5 Angle fillets				m				
6 Pointing in flashings				m	M5 Flashings are measured in Sections H70–H76		C4 Pointing in flashings is deemed to include cutting or forming grooves or chases	
7 Wedging and pinning	1 Width of wall stated			m			C5 Work is deemed to include preparation, cleaners, primers and sealers	S8 Type of filler and sealant S9 Method of application S10 Preparation of contact surfaces, cleaners, primers and sealers
8 Joints	1 Dimensioned description			m	M6 Joints are only measured where designed			
9 Slates and tiles for creasing	1 Width stated	1 Courses (nr)		m			C6 Slates and tiles for creasing and sills are deemed to include ends, angles and pointing	
10 Slate and tile sills				m				

CLASSIFICATION TABLE					MEASUREMENT RULES	DEFINITION RULES	COVERAGE RULES	SUPPLEMENTARY INFORMATION
11 Flue linings	1 Dimensioned description	m			M7 Brick flue linings are measured in Section F10:9.1.0.0		C7 Flue linings are deemed to include: (a) cutting to form easings (b) cutting to form bends (c) cutting to walls around linings	S11 Method of building
12 Air bricks 13 Ventilating gratings 14 Soot doors	1 Size of opening, nature and thickness of wall stated	nr	1 Lintels, details stated 2 Arches, details stated	nr			C8 Air bricks, ventilating gratings, soot doors and the like are deemed to include any necessary forming of openings, liners, cavity closers and damp proof courses	S12 Method of building
15 Gas flue blocks	1 Size of block and number of flues in each stated	nr						S12 Method of building
16 Proprietary items	1 Dimensioned description	nr	1 Manufacturer's reference	nr				S13 Method of fixing

G Structural/Carcassing metal/timber

G10 Structural steel framing
G11 Structural aluminium framing
G12 Isolated structural metal members

INFORMATION PROVIDED

P1 The following information is shown either on location drawings under A Preliminaries/General conditions or on further drawings which accompany the bills of quantities:
(a) the position of the work in relation to other parts of the work and of the proposed buildings
(b) the types and sizes of structural members and their positions in relation to each other
(c) details of connections or of the reactions, moments and axial loads at connection points

CLASSIFICATION TABLE

Classification				MEASUREMENT RULES	DEFINITION RULES	COVERAGE RULES	SUPPLEMENTARY INFORMATION
1 Framing, fabrication	1 Columns	1 Weight ≤ 40 kg/m	t	M1 The mass of framing includes all components except fittings	D1 Fabrication includes all operations up to and including delivery to site	C1 Items for fabrication measured by weight are deemed to include shop and site black bolts, nuts and washers for structural framing to structural framing connections	S1 Types and grades of materials
	2 Beams	2 Weight 40–100 kg/m		M2 Fittings are all grouped together irrespective of the member to which they are attached	D2 Purlins and cladding rails are measured by weight when hot rolled		S2 Details of welding tests and X-rays
	3 Bracings	3 Weight > 100 kg/m					S3 Details of performance tests
	4 Purlins and cladding rails	1 Castellated		M3 The mass of framing is measured from their overall lengths with no deductions for splay cuts or mitred ends or for the mass of metal removed to form notches and holes each < 0.10 m² in area measured in the plane	D3 Wires, cables, rods and bars include sag rods, ties and the like		
	5 Grillages	2 Tapered					
	6 Overhead crane rails	1 Details of fixing clips and resilient pads stated					
		3 Curved		M4 No allowance is made for the mass of weld fillets, black bolts, nuts, washers, rivets and protective coatings	D4 Special bolts and fasteners are those other than black bolts and holding down bolts or assemblies		
	7 Trestles, towers and built up columns	1 Details of construction stated					
	8 Trusses and built up girders	4 Cambered		M5 The mass of steel is taken for measurement as 785 kg/m² per 100 mm thickness (7.85 t/m³); the mass of other metals is stated			
	9 Wires, cables, rods and bars	5 Hollow, shape stated					
	10 Fittings						
	11 Holding down bolts or assemblies	1 Details stated	nr				
	12 Special bolts and fasteners	1 Type and diameter stated					

	First division	Second division	Third division	Unit	Rules
2 Framing, erection	1 Trial erection				D5 Erection includes all operations subsequent to fabrication
	2 Permanent erection on site			t	
3 Permanent formwork	1 Type and method of fixing stated			m²	D6 Permanent formwork is that which is structurally integral with the framing
4 Cold rolled purlins and cladding rails	1 Type and method of fixing stated			m	
5 Isolated structural member	1 Plain member use stated	1 Weight ≤ 40 kg/m 2 Weight 40–100 kg/m 3 Weight > 100 kg/m		t	D7 Use is defined as members is 1.1 – 1.9 inclusive
	2 Built-up member use and details of construction stated	1 Castellated 2 Tapered 3 Curved 4 Cambered 5 Hollow, shape stated			M6 The mass of built up members is calculated as defined from 'Framing, fabrication' M7 Fixing bolts are measured in accordance with the rules contained in Section G20:25.∗.0.0
	3 Fittings				D8 Fixing bolts are bolts fixing an isolated structural member to another element C2 Isolated structural members are deemed to include fabrication and erection
6 Filling hollow sections	1 Water				
	2 Concrete	1 Details stated		item	
7 Surface preparation	1 Blast cleaning 2 Pickling 3 Wire brushing 4 Flame cleaning 5 Others, details stated			m²	S4 Type of preparation, details of application and timing
8 Surface treatment	1 Galvanising 2 Sprayed metal coating 3 Protective painting 4 Others, details stated			m²	
9 Localised protective coating	1 Type stated			m²	M8 Localised protective coating is only measured to structural aluminium framing D9 Localised protective coatings are localised applications to surfaces in contact with dissimilar metals and aggressive building materials

INFORMATION PROVIDED

P1 The following information is shown either on location drawings under A Preliminaries/General conditions or on further drawings which accompany the bills of quantities:
(a) the scope and location of the work

CLASSIFICATION TABLE

Classification	Sub-classification	Dimension/detail	Unit	Further detail
1 Trusses 2 Trussed rafters 3 Trussed beams 4 Wall or partition panels 5 Portal frames		1 Dimensioned description	nr	1 Stopped labours (nr)
6 Floor members 7 Wall or partition members 8 Plates		1 Dimensioned description	m	1 Length > 6.00 m in one continuous length, length stated
9 Roof members	1 Flat 2 Pitched	1 Dimensioned description	m	
10 Joist strutting	1 Herringbone, depth of joist stated 2 Block, depth of joist stated	1 Dimensioned overall cross-section description and spacing of the members	m	
11 Butt jointed supports 12 Framed supports	1 Width > 300 mm	1 Dimensioned overall cross-section description	m²	1 Different cross-section shapes (nr) 2 Curved, radii stated 3 Stopped labours (nr) 4 Irregular shaped area 5 Irregular component, details stated
	2 Width ≤ 300 mm		m	
13 Individual supports		1 Dimensioned overall cross-section description	m	

MEASUREMENT RULES

M1 Strutting is measured over the joists

M2 Supports and framed supports are measured overall

DEFINITION RULES

D1 All sizes are nominal sizes unless stated as finished sizes

D2 Floor members include joists and beams

D3 Partition members include struts and noggings

D4 Plates are those to structural elements only and include bearers

D5 Flat roof members include joists and beams

D6 Pitched roof members include struts, purlins, rafters, hip and valley rafters, ridge boards, ceiling joists, binders and bracing

D7 Supports include grounds, battens, firrings, fillets, drips, rolls, upstands, kerbs or the like

D8 Framed supports are where the members are jointed together other than butt jointed

COVERAGE RULES

C1 The work is deemed to include labours on items of timber, except as otherwise required

C2 The work is deemed to include webs, gussets, etc.

SUPPLEMENTARY INFORMATION

S1 Kind and quality of materials and if timber is sawn or wrot

S2 Method of fixing where not at the discretion of the Contractor

S3 Fixing through vulnerable materials

S4 Preservative treatments applied as part of the production process

S5 Surface treatments applied as part of the production process

S6 Selection and protection for subsequent treatment

S7 Matching grain or colour

S8 Limits on the planing margins and if deviation from the stated sizes is not permitted

S9 Method of jointing or form of construction where not at the discretion of the Contractor

Item	Classification 1	Classification 2	Unit
14 Gutter boards	1 Width > 300 mm	1 Dimensioned description	m²
15 Fascia boards	2 Width > 300 mm	2 Dimensioned overall cross-section description	m
16 Eaves or verge soffit boards	3 Width ≤ 300 mm		
17 Cleats		1 Dimensioned description	nr
18 Ornamental ends		1 Dimensioned description	nr
19 Wrot surfaces	1 Plain	1 Width stated	m
	2 Irregular	1 Girth stated	m
20 Straps	1 Dimensioned description		nr
21 Hangers	2 Dimensioned diagram		
22 Shoes			
23 Nail plates			
24 Metal connectors			
25 Bolts			
26 Rod bracing			
27 Wire bracing			
28 Others, details stated			

Measurement rules

M3 Gutter boards and sides are each measured overall as individual components but grouped together

M4 The length of a bolt is measured overall the head

Definition rules

D9 Gutter boards include sides

D10 Fascia boards include barge boards

D11 Cleats include sprockets and the like

D12 Wrot surfaces are those on sawn items only

D13 Bolts include heads, nuts and washers

Coverage rules

C3 Work is deemed to include all labours in fabricating and fixing

C4 Work is deemed to include all accessories

68

INFORMATION PROVIDED

P1 The following information is shown either on drawings under A Preliminaries/General conditions or on further drawings which accompany the bills of quantities:
(a) the extent of the work and its height above ground level
(b) the size of units where not at the discretion of the Contractor

CLASSIFICATION TABLE

				MEASUREMENT RULES	DEFINITION RULES	COVERAGE RULES	SUPPLEMENTARY INFORMATION
1 Decking 2 Decking units (nr)	1 Dimensioned description		m²	1 Curved, radii stated 2 Fixing through underlinings	M1 The number is stated only where the size of unit is not at the discretion of the Contractor	D1 All sizes are nominal sizes unless stated as finished sizes	C1 Removal of lifting devices and consequent making good and making good of handling holes and the like are deemed to be included	S1 Kind and quality of materials S2 Method of fixing and hoisting where not at the discretion of the Contractor S3 Method of jointing or form of construction where not at the discretion of the Contractor S4 Surface treatments applied as part of the production process
3 Items extra over the decking or decking units in which they occur	1 Holes 2 Notches 3 Others, details stated	1 Off site 2 On site	nr	M2 No deduction is made for voids ≤ 0.50 m²			
4 Bearings 5 Eaves 6 Kerbs 7 Abutments 8 Nibs 9 Blocks 10 Fillets 11 Profile fillers	1 Dimensioned description		m				

INFORMATION PROVIDED

P1 The following information is shown either on location drawings under A Preliminaries/General conditions or on further drawings which accompany the bills of quantities:

(a) the extent of the work and its height above ground level

(b) the size of units where not at the discretion of the Contractor

CLASSIFICATION TABLE

					MEASUREMENT RULES	DEFINITION RULES	COVERAGE RULES	SUPPLEMENTARY INFORMATION
1 Decking		1 Dimensioned description		m²		D1 All sizes are nominal sizes unless stated as finished sizes	C1 Removal of lifting devices and consequent making good, and making good of handling holes and the like are deemed to be included	S1 Kind and quality of materials and whether sawn or wrot
2 Decking units (nr)				nr				S2 Method of fixing and hoisting where not at the discretion of the Contractor
3 Items extra over the decking or decking units in which they occur	1 Holes	1 Off site		nr	M1 The number is stated only where the size of unit is not at the discretion of the Contractor			S3 Method of jointing or form of construction where not at the discretion of the Contractor
	2 Notches	2 On site			M2 No deduction is made for voids ≤ 0.50 m²			S4 Selection and protection for subsequent treatment
	3 Others, details stated							S5 Surface treatments applied as part of the production process
4 Woodwool kerbs	1 Dimensioned description			m	M3 Items 4–7.*.0.* are only measured under Section G32			S6 Matching grain or colour
5 Woodwool angle fillets								S7 Limits on the planing margins and if deviation from the stated sizes is not permitted
6 Filling rebates with insulating strips								
7 Isolating strips		1 Curved, radii stated						

H Cladding/Covering

H10 Patent glazing
H12 Plastics glazed vaulting/walling
H13 Structural glass assemblies

	MEASUREMENT RULES	DEFINITION RULES	COVERAGE RULES	SUPPLEMENTARY INFORMATION
INFORMATION PROVIDED P1 The following information is shown either on location drawings under A Preliminaries/General conditions or on further drawings which accompany the bills of quantities: (a) the scope and location of the work (b) component drawings	M1 No deduction is made for voids ≤ 1.00 m²			

CLASSIFICATION TABLE

					MEASUREMENT RULES	DEFINITION RULES	COVERAGE RULES	SUPPLEMENTARY INFORMATION
1 Single tier 2 Multi-tier		m²	1 Site drilling the bearings		M2 Glazing is measured over bars		C1 Work is deemed to include securing to wood unless otherwise stated	S1 Kind, quality and thickness of materials S2 Type, finish, length and spacing of glazing members S3 Nature, thickness and spacing of structural supports
3 Items extra over the glazing in which they occur	1 Doors 2 Windows 3 Fixed louvres 4 Adjustable louvres 5 Others, details stated	nr	1 Dimensioned description	1 Control gear to single unit, type, method of fixing and distance vertically and horizontally from unit stated 2 Control gear to bank of units, type, method of fixing and distance vertically and horizontally from units stated				
4 Raking cutting 5 Curved cutting		m	1 Dimensioned description	1 Site drilling, background stated	M3 Labours on glazing are grouped with the glazing to which they relate		C2 Stop ends, mitres and corners are deemed to be included	
6 Weatherings, flashings and fixing members at tops, bottoms and sides where part of the component	1 Preformed, gauge stated 2 Extruded, thickness stated	m	1 Dimensioned description					

INFORMATION PROVIDED

P1 The following information is shown either on location drawings under A Preliminaries/General conditions or on further drawings which accompany the bills of quantities:
(a) the scope and location of the work
(b) component drawings

CLASSIFICATION TABLE

					MEASUREMENT RULES	DEFINITION RULES	COVERAGE RULES	SUPPLEMENTARY INFORMATION
1 Curtain walling					M1 Timber members which do not have a constant cross-section are so described and given stating the extreme dimensions	D1 Curtain walling comprises non loadbearing walls of wood or metal framing, fixed as an intergrated assembly, complete with windows and opening lights, glazing and infill panels	C1 Curtain walling is deemed to include all cleats, brackets, bolts and fixings	S1 Kind and quality of materials and if timber whether sawn or wrot
2 Items extra over the curtain walling in which they occur					M2 No deduction is made for voids ≤ 1.00 m²	D2 All sizes are nominal sizes unless stated as finished sizes		S2 Preservative treatments applied as part of the production process
	1 Infill panels	1 Type and thickness stated	1 Flat	m²	M3 Infill panels are measured over all framing		C2 Items include:	S3 Surface treatments applied as part of the production process
			2 Sloping				(a) doors where supplied with the unit	S4 Selection and protection for subsequent treatment
			3 Curved, radii stated				(b) architraves, trims and the like where part of the component	S5 Matching grain or colour
	2 Perimeter	1 Dimensioned description	1 Heads	m		D3 Irregular junctions are any junctions with angles other than 90°	(c) ironmongery where supplied with the component	S6 Limits on planing margins on timber and if deviation from stated size is not permitted
			2 Sills				(d) finishes where part of the component	S7 Method of jointing or form of construction
			3 Abutments				(e) glazing where supplied with the component	S8 Thickness or substance
	3 Angle	1 Internal	1 Irregular	m			(f) mechanical operation and automatic operating equipment where supplied with the component	S9 Method of fixing where not at the discretion of the Contractor
		2 External	2 Horizontal				(g) mastics/sealants unless executed by a specialist and measured in Section P22	S10 Bedding and jointing or pointing compound
			3 Sloping				(h) fixings and tastenings	S11 Fixing through vulnerable materials
			4 Vertical					
			5 Curved, radii stated					
	4 Closer	1 Fire stops		nr				
		2 Partition closer						
		3 Angle closer						
		4 Plaster stop						
	5 Opening lights	1 Dimensioned description		nr		D4 Opening lights include opening gear as appropriate		
	6 Doors							

INFORMATION PROVIDED				MEASUREMENT RULES	DEFINITION RULES	COVERAGE RULES	SUPPLEMENTARY INFORMATION
P1 Information is shown on location drawings under A Preliminaries/General conditions							
CLASSIFICATION TABLE							
1 Rooflights	1 Dimensioned description (nr)	1 Sizes and extent of reinforcement stated	m²	M1 Isolated glass lenses are measured in Section E42		C1 Roof and pavement lights are deemed to include moulds, formwork, reinforcement, bedding and glass lenses	S1 Kind and quality of materials
2 Pavement lights	2 Dimensioned description						S2 Bedding and fixing
3 Vertical units			nr				S3 Surface finishes
4 Joints	1 Dimensioned description	1 Sizes of filling and sealants stated	m				

H20 Rigid sheet cladding

H21 Timber weatherboarding

K11 Rigid sheet flooring/sheathing/linings/casings

K12 Under purlin/inside rail panel linings

K13 Rigid sheet fine linings/panelling

K20 Timber board flooring/sheathing/linings/casings

K21 Timber narrow strip flooring/linings/linings

INFORMATION PROVIDED	MEASUREMENT RULES	DEFINITION RULES	COVERAGE RULES	SUPPLEMENTARY INFORMATION
P1 Information is shown on location drawings under A Preliminaries/General conditions	M1 No deduction is made for voids ≤ 0.50 m²	D1 The work is deemed internal unless described as external	C1 The work is deemed to include:	
	M2 Work to ceilings and beams over 3.50 m above floor (measured to ceiling level in both cases), is so described stating the height in further 1.50 m stages	D2 All sizes are nominal sizes unless stated as finished sizes	(a) labours, except as otherwise required	
		D3 Timber items which do not have a constant cross-section are so described and given stating the extreme dimensions	(b) breather paper lining/sheathing	
			(c) angles, except as otherwise required	

CLASSIFICATION TABLE

Classification	Sub-classification		Measured	Unit	Measurement rules	Definition & Supplementary rules
1 Walls 2 Floors 3 Ceilings 4 Roofs 5 Tops and cheeks of dormers	1 Width > 300 mm	1 Dimensioned description		m²	M3 Width stages are measured the width of each recesses in walls and attached columns face	D4 Walls include jambs and cills to openings and recesses in walls and attached columns
	2 Width ≤ 300 mm			m		D5 Ceilings include soffits to openings and recesses in walls, all faces of recesses in ceilings and attached beams
	3 Area ≤ 1.00 m², irrespective of width		1 Laid diagonally 2 Sloping 3 Curved, radii stated 4 Obstructed by integral services	nr		D6 Sloping is defined as sloping both > 10° from horizontal and > 10° from vertical
6 Isolated beams 7 Isolated columns	1 Total girth ≤ 600 mm 2 and thereafter in 600 mm stages			m²	M4 The girth is measured on the external finished face	D7 Isolated beams and isolated columns include the faces of attached beams and attached columns which have a different finish from the adjoining face
8 Abutments	1 Type stated			m		D8 Abutments are defined as being where the detail is different from the standard detail and (where appropriate) include around openings etc.
9 Finished angles	1 External 2 Internal			m		D9 Finished angles are those where the decorative veneer or facing is returned or on panelling where angles are other than butt jointed
10 Holes				nr		D10 Holes are those for pipes, standards and the like
11 Fire stops	1 Dimensioned description			m		
12 Items extra over the work in which they occur	1 Access panels	1 Dimensioned description		nr		

S1 Type, quality and thickness of materials and if timber whether sawn or wrot
S2 Method of jointing or form of construction where not at the discretion of the Contractor
S3 Nature of background
S4 Preservative treatments applied as part of the production process
S5 Surface treatments applied as part of the production process
S6 Fire retardant treatments
S7 Details of cover and jointing strips and cover mouldings
S8 Selection and protection for subsequent treatments
S9 Constraints on width of board and planing margins and limitations if deviation from stated sizes is not permitted
S10 Matching grain or colour
S11 Fixing through vulnerable materials
S12 Method of fixing where not at the discretion of the Contractor
S13 Details of finish, trim or support

H30 Fibre cement profiled sheet cladding/covering/siding
H31 Metal profiled/flat sheet cladding/covering/siding
H32 Plastics profiled sheet cladding/covering/siding
H33 Bitumen and fibre profiled sheet cladding/covering
H41 Glass reinforced plastics cladding/covering/features

INFORMATION PROVIDED

P1 The following information is shown either on location drawings under A Preliminaries/General conditions or on further drawings which accompany the bills of quantities:

(a) the extent of the work and its height above ground level

CLASSIFICATION TABLE

			MEASUREMENT RULES	DEFINITION RULES	COVERAGE RULES	SUPPLEMENTARY INFORMATION
1 Roof coverings 1 Pitch stated 2 Wall cladding	1 Curved, radii stated 2 Fixed through underlinings	m²	M1 No deduction is made for voids ≤ 1.00 m²		C1 Coverings are deemed to include: (a) work in forming voids ≤ 1.00 m² other than holes (b) integral underlay	S1 Kind, quality and size of materials S2 Type and spacing of fixing S3 Minimum side and end laps S4 Jointing or sealing S5 Nature, thickness and spacing of structural supports
3 Abutments 4 Eaves 5 Verges 6 Ridges 7 Hips 8 Vertical angles 9 Valleys 10 Expansion joints 11 Barge boards 12 Skirtings 13 Flashings 14 Aprons/sills 15 Gutters and linings 16 Jambs 17 Filler pieces	1 Dimensioned cross-section description	m 1 Raking 2 Curved, radii stated	M2 Boundary work to voids is only measured where the void is > 1.00 m²		C2 Boundary work is deemed to include bedding, pointing, ends, angles and intersections	

18 Items extra over roof coverings	1 Translucent sheets	1 Dimensioned description	nr
	2 Sheets with soaker flanges		
	3 Rooflight units		
	4 Sheets with louvre blades		
	5 Ventilators		
	6 Junctions		
19 Items extra over wall cladding			
20 Cutting	1 Raking		m
	2 Curved		nr
21 Holes	1 Dimensioned description		m
22 Fire stops	1 Dimensioned description		

D1 Holes are those for pipes, standards and the like

INFORMATION PROVIDED

P1 The following information is shown either on location drawings which accompany the bills of quantities under A Preliminaries/General conditions or on further drawings:

(a) the scope and location of the work

CLASSIFICATION TABLE

Classification (1st)	Classification (2nd)	Classification (3rd)	Unit	MEASUREMENT RULES	DEFINITION RULES	COVERAGE RULES	SUPPLEMENTARY INFORMATION
1 Walls 2 Ceilings 3 Isolated beams 4 Isolated columns	1 Plain, width > 300 mm 2 Plain, width ≤ 300 mm	1 Patterned, details stated	m²	M1 Work is measured on the exposed face and no deduction is made for voids ≤ 0.50 m²	D1 All work is deemed as external unless described as internal	C1 The work is deemed to include: (a) fair joints (b) working over and around obstructions (c) additional labour for overhand work (d) cutting (e) drainage holes (f) bedding mortars and adhesives (g) grouting (h) cleaning, sealing and polishing	S1 Kind and quality of materials S2 Size, shape and thickness of units S3 Nature of base S4 Preparatory work S5 Nature of finished surface including any sealing/polishing S6 Bedding or other method of fixing S7 Treatment of joints S8 Layout of joints
	3 Work with joints laid out to detail, width > 300 mm 4 Work with joints laid out to detail, width ≤ 300 mm	1 Dimensioned description	m²	M2 Work in staircase areas and plant rooms are each given separately	D2 The thickness stated is the thickness exclusive of keys, grooves and the like given separately	C2 Work to walls, ceilings, beams and columns is deemed to include internal and external angles and intersections ≤ 10 mm radius	
			m	M3 Work to ceilings and beams over 3.50 m above floor (measured to ceiling level in both cases), except in staircase areas, is so described stating the height in further 1.50 m stages	D3 Rounded internal and external angles > 10 mm radius are classified as curved work where not measured under 15.1.*.0	C3 Work to floors is deemed to include intersections in sloping work	
5 Floors	1 Level or to falls only ≤ 15° from horizontal 2 To falls and crossfalls and to slopes ≤ 15° from horizontal 3 To slopes > 15° from horizontal	1 Plain 2 Work with joints laid out to detail, dimensioned diagram stated	m²	M4 Curved work is so described with the radii stated measured on face	D4 Beams and columns are classified as isolated where the work is different from the abutting ceilings or walls		
		1 Patterned work, details stated 2 Floors laid in bays, average size of bays stated 3 Inserts, size or section stated	m	M5 Width is the width of each face	D5 Work to sides and soffits of attached beams and openings and to sides of attached columns is classed as work to the abutting walls or ceilings		
					D6 Floors include landings		

Item	Classification	Sub-division	Further sub-division	Unit	
6 Treads		1 Width stated		m	
7 Sills					
8 Risers	1 Plain 2 Undercut	1 Height stated	1 Undercut	m	
9 Strings					
10 Aprons					
11 Linings to channels	1 Horizontal 2 To falls	1 Girth on face stated	1 Patterned work, details stated 2 Inserts, size or section stated 3 Flush 4 Raking 5 Vertical	m	
12 Skirtings	1 Height stated			m	
13 Kerbs	2 Height and width stated				
14 Corner pieces		1 Dimensioned description		nr	
15 Items extra over the work in which they occur		1 Special units		m	
		2 Manufacturer's reference		nr	
16 Accessories	1 Separating membranes, thickness stated			m²	
	2 Movement joints	1 Dimensioned description		m	
	3 Cover strips	1 In situ		nr	
	4 Dividing strips	2 Precast	1 Undercut		
	5 Ornaments, dimensioned description and character stated			nr	
	6 Fixings, details stated				

C4 Work to treads, sills and risers is deemed to include fair edges, internal and external angles

C5 Curved treads, risers, strings and aprons are deemed to include curved and radiused cutting for special edge tiles

C6 Strings and aprons are deemed to include fair edges, ends, angles and ramps

C7 Linings to channels are deemed to include fair edges, ends, angles, intersections and outlets

C8 Skirtings and kerbs are deemed to include fair edges, rounded edges, ends, angles and ramps

D7 Special units include non-standard units to produce fair edges, internal and external angles, moulded edges, beaded edges, and coved junctions

D8 Movement joints include expansion joints

D9 Ornaments are irregularly occurring features

S9 Method of fixing

H60 Clay/concrete roof tiling
H61 Fibre cement slating
H62 Natural slating
H63 Reconstructed stone slating/tiling
H64 Timber shingling

INFORMATION PROVIDED

P1 The following information is shown either on location drawings under A Preliminaries/General conditions or on further drawings which accompany the bills of quantities:
(a) the extent of the roofing work and its height above ground level

CLASSIFICATION TABLE

				MEASUREMENT RULES	DEFINITION RULES	COVERAGE RULES	SUPPLEMENTARY INFORMATION
1 Roof coverings	1 Pitch stated	m²	1 Curved, radii stated	M1 No deduction is made for voids ≤ 1.00 m²		C1 Coverings are deemed to include: (a) underlay and battens (b) work in forming voids ≤ 1.00 m² other than holes	S1 Kind, quality and size of materials
2 Wall coverings							S2 Method of fixing
							S3 Minimum laps
							S4 Spacing of battens and counter battens
3 Abutments		m	1 Raking	M2 Boundary work to voids is only measured where the void is > 1.00 m²		C2 Boundary work is deemed to include undercloaks, cutting, bedding, pointing, ends, angles and intersections	S5 Method of forming
4 Eaves			2 Curved, radii stated				
5 Verges							
6 Ridges							
7 Hips							
8 Vertical angles							
9 Valleys							
10 Fittings	1 Ventilators 2 Finials 3 Gas terminals 4 Hip irons 5 Soakers 6 Saddles	nr	1 Dimensioned description				
11 Holes		nr	1 Fixing only		D1 Holes are those for pipes, standards and the like		

H70 Malleable metal sheet prebonded coverings/cladding
H71 Lead sheet coverings/flashings
H72 Aluminium sheet coverings/flashings
H73 Copper sheet coverings/flashings
H74 Zinc sheet coverings/flashings
H75 Stainless steel sheet coverings/flashings
H76 Fibre bitumen thermoplastic sheet coverings/flashings

INFORMATION PROVIDED	MEASUREMENT RULES	DEFINITION RULES	COVERAGE RULES	SUPPLEMENTARY INFORMATION
P1 The following information is shown either on location drawings under A Preliminaries/General conditions or on further drawings which accompany the bills of quantities: (a) the extent of the roofing work and its height above ground level (b) the location and spacing of all laps, drips, welts, beads, seams, rolls, upstands and downstands	M1 No deduction is made for voids ≤ 1.00 m² M2 The following allowances are made in calculating the area to be measured: (a) 180 mm for each drip < 50 mm high (b) 80 mm for each welt (c) 250 mm for each roll < 50 mm high (d) 100 mm for each seam < 50 mm high (e) 500 mm for each lap (f) 500 mm for each upstand/downstand		C1 Coverings are deemed to include: (a) isolated areas (b) work to falls and crossfalls (c) underlay in contact with the covering (d) work in forming voids ≤ 1.00 m² other than holes (e) dressing/wedging into grooves, hollows, recesses and the like	S1 Type and quality of materials for backing, underlays, coverings, cladding and flashings S2 Thickness, weight and temper grade S3 Method of fixing S4 Details of laps, drips, welts, beads, rolls, joints, upstands and downstands S5 Type of support materials S6 Special finishes

CLASSIFICATION TABLE

1 Roof coverings 2 Wall coverings 3 Preformed cladding panels 4 Dormers 5 Hoods 6 Domes 7 Spires 8 Finials 9 Soffits	1 Pitch stated	1 Curved, radii stated	m²

CLASSIFICATION TABLE

				Unit	MEASUREMENT RULES	DEFINITION RULES	COVERAGE RULES	SUPPLEMENTARY INFORMATION
10 Flashings 11 Aprons 12 Sills 13 Weatherings 14 Cappings 15 Hips 16 Kerbs 17 Ridges 18 Reveals, returns and jambs	1 Dimensioned description 2 Dimensioned diagram	1 Horizontal 2 Sloping 3 Vertical 4 Stepped 5 Preformed 6 Dressing over corrugated roofing 7 Dressing over slating and tiling 8 Dressing over glass and glazing bars		m	M3 Boundary work to voids is only measured where the void is > 1.00 m²		C2 Work is deemed to include: (a) laps, seams, ends (b) angles and intersections (c) rolls (d) upstands and downstands (e) dressing/wedging into grooves, hollows, recesses and the like	
19 Gutters	1 Dimensioned description	1 Stepped 2 Secret 3 Sloping 4 Tapered 5 Preformed		m				
20 Catchpits 21 Sumps 22 Outlets	1 Dimensioned description			nr				
23 Edges	1 Welted 2 Beaded 3 Shaped			m				
24 Dressings	1 Corrugated roofing 2 Slating and tiling 3 Glass and glazing bars	1 Nature of roofing	1 Down corrugations 2 Across corrugations	m				
25 Saddles 26 Soakers and slates 27 Hatch covers 28 Ventilators	1 Dimensioned description	1 Handed to others for fixing		nr		D1 Collars include pipe sleeves		
29 Collars around pipes, standards and the like	1 Size of member and length of collar stated			nr			C3 All dressing and bossing is deemed included	
30 Holes				nr		D2 Holes are those for pipes, standards and the like		

1 Details stated

J Waterproofing

J20 Mastic asphalt tanking/damp proof membranes
J21 Mastic asphalt roofing/insulation/finishes
J22 Proprietary roof decking with asphalt finish
J30 Liquid applied tanking/damp proof membranes
J31 Liquid applied waterproof roof coatings
M11 Mastic asphalt flooring

INFORMATION PROVIDED

P1 The following information is shown either on location drawings under A Preliminaries/General conditions or on further drawings which accompany the bills of quantities:

(a) plan of each level indicating the extent of the work and its height above ground level together with restrictions on the siting of plant and materials

(b) section indicating the extent of tanking work

		MEASUREMENT RULES	DEFINITION RULES	COVERAGE RULES	SUPPLEMENTARY INFORMATION
		M1 Mastic asphalt flooring in staircase areas and plant areas and plant rooms are each given separately			
		M2 Curved work is so described	D1 Mastic asphalt flooring is deemed internal unless described as external	C1 Work is deemed to include:	S1 Kind, quality and size of materials including underlays and reinforcement
				(a) cutting to line	S2 Thickness and number of coats
				(b) cutting, notching, bending and extra material for lapping the underlay and reinforcement	S3 Nature of base on which applied
				(c) working into recessed duct covers and the like, shaped insets, recessed manhole covers, mat sinkings, outlet pipes, dishing to gullies and the like	S4 Surface treatments
				(d) work to falls and crossfalls	S5 Method of fixing decking
					S6 Spacing of structural supports

CLASSIFICATION TABLE

1 Tanking and damp proofing	1 Width ≤ 150 mm			
2 Flooring and underlay	2 Width 150 – 225 mm			
3 Roofing	3 Width 225 – 300 mm	1 Pitch stated		
4 Paving	4 Width > 300 mm			
		m²	1 Work subsequently covered	
			2 Carried out in working space ≤ 600 mm wide	M3 The area measured is that in contact with the base and no deduction is made for voids ≤ 1.00 m²
			3 Overhand work	
				C2 Work is deemed to include:
				(a) working to metal or other flashings and working against frames of manhole covers, duct covers and the like
				(b) intersections on work to crossfalls
				C3 Work subsequently covered is deemed to include edges and arrises

Classification	First sub	Second sub	Unit	Supplementary	Measurement rules	Definition rules	Coverage rules
5 Skirtings 6 Fascias 7 Aprons	1 Girth ≤ 150 mm 2 Girth 150 – 225 mm 3 Girth 225 – 300 mm 4 Girth > 300 mm girth stated	1 Stepped 2 Raking 3 Raking in two planes	m		M4 Girth is measured on face M5 Boundary work to voids is only measured where the void is > 1.00 m²		C4 Skirtings, fascias and aprons are deemed to include edges, drips, arrises, internal angle-fillets, dressing over tilting fillets, turning nibs into grooves, angles, stopped ends requiring angle fillets, stopped ends, fair ends, and extra materials for turning into grooves
8 Linings to gutters 9 Linings to channels 10 Linings to valleys 11 Coverings to kerbs							C5 Linings to gutters, channels and valleys and coverings to kerbs are deemed to include edges, arrises, internal angle-fillets, tilting fillets, turning nibs into grooves, ends, angles, intersections, outlets and extra material for turning into grooves
12 Internal angle fillets	1 Dimensioned description		m	1 Coats (nr) where other than two			C6 Internal angle fillets are deemed to include ends and angles
13 Fair edges 14 Rounded edges 15 Drips 16 Arrises 17 Turning asphalt nibs into grooves			m		M6 12-17.*.0.* are only measured in association with work measured under 1–4.*.1.* M7 Edges and arrises are only measured separately where the work is not subsequently covered		
18 Collars around pipes, standards and like members	1 Size of member and length of collar stated		nr			D2 Collars include pipe sleeves	C7 Collars around pipes, standards and the like are deemed to include arrises and internal angle fillets
19 Linings to cesspools 20 Linings to sumps 21 Linings to manholes	1 Dimensioned description		nr				C8 Linings to cesspools, sumps and the like are deemed to include arrises, internal angle-fillets and outlets
22 Edge trim			m			D3 Edge trim includes preformed angle trim	C9 Edge trim is deemed to include ends, angles and intersections
23 Roof ventilators			nr				

J40 Flexible sheet tanking/damp proof membranes
J41 Built up felt roof coverings
J42 Single layer plastics roof coverings
J43 Proprietary roof decking with felt finish

INFORMATION PROVIDED

P1 The following information is shown either on location drawings under A Preliminaries/General conditions or on further drawings which accompany the bills of quantities:

(a) plan at each level indicating the extent of the work and its height above ground level together with restrictions on the siting of plant and materials

CLASSIFICATION TABLE

Classification				Unit	MEASUREMENT RULES	DEFINITION RULES	COVERAGE RULES	SUPPLEMENTARY INFORMATION
1 Tanking and damp proofing	1 Pitch stated			m²	M1 Curved work is so described with the radii stated		C1 Work is deemed to include: (a) cutting and fair edges applied (b) notching, bending and extra material for laps	S1 Kind, quality and size of materials including underlays
2 Roof coverings	1 Curved radii stated			m²	M2 The area measured is that in contact with the base and no deduction is made for voids ≤ 1.00 m²			S2 Nature of base on which applied
3 Abutments	1 Girth > 2.00 m	1 Raking		m²	M3 Boundary work to voids is only measured where the void is > 1.00 m²		C2 Boundary work is deemed to include all cutting, ends, angles, intersections, notching, bending, turning into grooves, wedging, dressing, trimming and jointing covering to flashings, working into channels and the like and filler pieces	S3 Method of jointing
4 Eaves	2 Girth ≤ 2.00 m in 200 mm stages	2 Stepped		m				S4 Method of fixing decking
5 Verges								S5 Spacing of structural supports
6 Ridges								
7 Hips								
8 Vertical angles								
9 Valleys								
10 Skirtings								
11 Flashings								
12 Aprons								
13 Gutters and linings								
14 Coverings to kerbs	1 Dimensioned description							
15 Linings to cesspools	1 Dimensioned description			nr		D1 Collars include pipe sleeves		
16 Linings to sumps	1 Dimensioned description							
17 Collars around pipes, standards and the like	1 Size of pipe and length of collar stated							
18 Outlets and dishing to gullies	1 Dimensioned description							

	1 Dimensioned description		
19 Edge trim		m	D2 Edge trim includes preformed angle trim / C3 Edge trim is deemed to include ends, angles and intersections
20 Roof ventilators		nr	
21 Holes		nr	D3 Holes are those for pipes, standards and the like
22 Fire stops		m	

K Linings/Sheathing/Dry partitioning

K10 Plasterboard dry lining
K31 Plasterboard fixed partitions/inner walls/linings

INFORMATION PROVIDED	MEASUREMENT RULES	DEFINITION RULES	COVERAGE RULES	SUPPLEMENTARY INFORMATION
P1 The following information is shown either on location drawings under A Preliminaries/General conditions or on further drawings which accompany the bills of quantities: (a) the scope and location of the work (b) the services located within the ceiling or partition where the work includes complex integral services	M1 Work in staircase areas and plant rooms are each given separately M2 Work to ceilings and beams over 3.50 m above floor (measured to ceiling level in both cases), except in staircase areas, is so described stating the height in further 1.50 m stages. M3 Insulation, vapour barriers, fire barriers, isolating membranes, moisture resistant treatment and the like, are only measured in this section where they are an integral part of a lining, or partition or ceiling, or are fixed thereto	D1 Work is deemed internal unless described as external	C1 Work is deemed to include: (a) fair joints (b) working over and around obstructions into recesses and shaped inserts (c) additional labour for overhand work (d) plaster for dabs, filling and finishing (e) joint and reinforcing tape (f) bitumen impregnated pads C2 Patterned work is deemed to include all extra work involved	S1 Kind, quality and thickness of sheeting and components S2 Method of construction S3 Layout and treatment of joints S4 Complex integral services S5 Method of fixing S6 Thermal insulation and vapour barriers fixed with lining S7 Insulation to limit sound transmission S8 Moisture resistant treatment and the like S9 Surface applications forming part of dry lining S10 Isolating membranes S11 Method of jointing composite panels

CLASSIFICATION TABLE

			Unit		Measurement rules	Definition / Coverage / Supplementary rules
1 Proprietary partitions	1 Height in 300 mm stages and thickness of partition stated	1 Boarded one side	m		M4 The work is measured over obstructions	C3 Partitions and linings are deemed to include the following where part of the proprietary system they are deemed to include the following. Where not a part of the proprietary system they are measured in accordance with the appropriate Work Section rules:
		2 Boarded both sides	m		M5 No allowance is made in measurement for lapped joints	(a) head and sole plates
2 Linings	1 Walls	1 Height in 300 mm stages stated	m	1 Patterned, details stated	M6 The linear measurement of partitions is the mean length of the partition	(b) studs, stiffening sections, firrings and channels
	2 Beams, faces (nr)	1 Total girth ≤ 600 mm	m	2 Curved, radii stated	M7 The linear measurement of linings is the length on face	(c) metal resilient bars
	3 Columns, faces (nr)	2 and thereafter in 600 mm stages		3 Obstructed by integral services	M8 No deduction is made for voids in partitions and linings measured linearly other than for those voids which extend full height, full girth or full width	(d) jointing battens
	4 Reveals and soffits of openings and recesses	1 Width ≤ 300 mm	m		M9 No deduction is made for voids ≤ 0.50 m² in linings measured superficially	(e) insulation and barriers
		2 Width 300 – 600 mm			M10 Where one face of a double sided partition or a face of lining is carried across the surface of an obstruction, the partition or lining is measured overall and no item of abutments is measured	(f) fillets, battens and the like
	5 Ceilings		m²		M11 A recess is only measured where it is for part only of the height and not where it is full height	D2 The height of framed work is the height of the frame and where the heights of the boarding differ then this is so stated giving details
3 Angles to partitions	1 Thickness of partition stated		m			D3 Reveals and soffits of openings and recesses in linings > 600 mm are defined as to walls, beams or columns
4 Tee junctions to partitions	1 Thickness of partition stated		m			D4 Linings are those which do not form part of a proprietary system and exclude timber framing
5 Crosses to partitions	1 Plain		m	1 Between different forms of construction, finish details stated		D5 Abutments include trimming to openings which extend full height, full width or full girth or finished with the same finish as the faces. Trimming to openings which are not full height, full girth or full width are deemed to be included
6 Abutments	2 Irregular		m			C4 Angles, tee junctions, crosses and abutments are deemed to include the extra work involved, studding, grounds, angle tapes and the like
7 Angles to linings	1 Thickness of partition or lining stated	1 Internal	m			C5 Angles are deemed to include the extra work involved, angle tapes and the like
		2 External	m			
		1 Between different board finishes, details stated				S12 Detail of finish or trim, grounds or framing

CLASSIFICATION TABLE				MEASUREMENT RULES	DEFINITION RULES	COVERAGE RULES	SUPPLEMENTARY INFORMATION
8 Fair ends to partitions	1 Thickness of partition stated		m	M12 Fair ends are only measured where the exposed end of the partition is finished with the same finish as the faces, or with a trim which is an integral part of the partition system	D6 Fair ends to partitions include trimming to openings	C6 Fair ends are deemed to include the extra work involved, studding, boarding, trims and the like	S13 Details of finish or trim
9 Beads, function stated		1 Dimensioned description	m		D7 The function of beads as angle beads, casing beads, trims and the like are stated	C7 Beads are deemed to include working finishes thereto	
10 Fixings for heavy fittings	1 Sinks 2 Radiators 3 Cupboards 4 Others, details stated		nr		D8 Heavy fittings are those requiring additional support	C8 Fixings for heavy fittings are deemed to include additional supports and any cutting of boarding, trim or jointing	S14 Type of additional supports
11 Items extra over the work in which they occur	1 Access panels		nr				S15 Type of panels

INFORMATION PROVIDED

P1 The following information is shown either on location drawings under A Preliminaries/General conditions or on further drawings which accompany the bills of quantities:
(a) the scope and location of the work
(b) the services located within the partition

CLASSIFICATION TABLE

Classification				MEASUREMENT RULES	DEFINITION RULES	COVERAGE RULES	SUPPLEMENTARY INFORMATION
1 Partitions	1 Height and thickness of partition stated	1 Factory applied finish	m	M1 The work is measured over the obstructions	D1 Work is deemed internal unless described as external	C1 Partitions are deemed to include all integral components, holes, etc	S1 Kind and quality of materials
		2 Site applied finish	m	M2 The linear measurement of partitions is the mean length of the partition			S2 Method of construction
		1 Curved, radii stated		M3 Factory applied finishes and site applied finishes are only measured where not at the discretion of the Contractor			S3 Layout of joints
		2 Obstructed by integral services					S4 Method of fixing
							S5 Complex integral services
2 Trims	1 Dimensioned description		m		D2 Trims are separate items fixed on site as cover pieces to edges or panel joints		
3 Openings, extra over the partitions in which they occur	1 Blanks	1 Dimensioned description	nr		D3 Openings is a general term for breaks in the general construction of partitions and includes the components filling the openings	C2 Openings are deemed to include additional integral components	
	2 Doors					C3 Openings are deemed to include ironmongery, glass, linings or the like but exclude trim	S6 Method of bedding, jointing or pointing
	3 Windows						S7 Details of ironmongery, glass, linings or the like
	4 Glazed panels						
	5 Access panels						

K32 Framed panel cubicle partitions

INFORMATION PROVIDED

P1 The following information is shown either on location drawings under A Preliminaries/General conditions or on further drawings which accompany the bills of quantities:

(a) the scope and location of the work

CLASSIFICATION TABLE

				MEASUREMENT RULES	DEFINITION RULES	COVERAGE RULES	SUPPLEMENTARY INFORMATION
1 Cubicle partitions; set	1 Dimensioned diagram		nr		D1 Cubicle partitions include doors, ironmongery or the like but exclude trims	C1 Cubicle partitions are deemed to include framing, stiffening, connecting and fixing devices supporting legs and brackets	S1 Kind and quality of materials
2 Trim	1 Dimensioned description		m		D2 Trims refer to separate items fixed on site at junction of cubicles and at junctions with adjoining constructions		S2 Method of construction
							S3 Method of fixing
							S4 Method of bedding, jointing or pointing

K40 Suspended ceilings

INFORMATION PROVIDED

P1 The following information is shown either on location drawings under A Preliminaries/General conditions or on further drawings which accompany the bills of quantities:
(a) the scope and location of the work including integral fittings
(b) the services located within the suspended ceiling void including any additional support for same

CLASSIFICATION TABLE

				MEASUREMENT RULES	DEFINITION RULES	COVERAGE RULES	SUPPLEMENTARY INFORMATION
1 Ceilings 2 Beams	1 Depth of suspension ≤ 150 mm 2 Depth of suspension 150 – 500 mm 3 and thereafter in 500 mm stages	1 Thickness of lining and method of fixing system to structure stated	m²	M1 Soffit linings on battens, etc. fixed direct to underside of slab are measured elsewhere in the relevant Sections	D1 All work is deemed internal unless described as external	C1 Suspended ceilings etc. are deemed to include: (a) working over and around obstructions (b) support work and accessories for fittings (c) suspension and framed members	S1 Kind and quality of materials S2 Size of panels and strips S3 Construction of framing and suspension systems S4 Method of fixing S5 Nature of backgrounds S6 Services in the suspended ceiling void S7 Insulation materials S8 Vapour barriers S9 Integral heating, ventilation, lighting and fire prevention fittings
		1 Patterned, details stated 2 Sloping linings, details stated 3 Curved, radii stated 4 Suspension obstructed by services 5 Trims at regular intervals within area of suspended ceiling, details stated		M2 Work in staircase areas and plant rooms are each given separately	D2 Integral fittings occur where the fittings are designed and incorporated into the ceiling structure	C2 Patterned work is deemed to include all extra work involved	
				M3 Work to ceilings and beams over 3.50 m above floor (measured to ceiling level in both cases), except in staircase areas, is so described stating the height in further 1.50 m stages		C3 Work incorporating integral fittings is deemed to include additional hangers, framing and the like	
				M4 The area measured is that on the exposed face and no deduction is made for voids ≤ 0.50 m²			
				M5 The depth of suspension is measured from the main structural soffit to the lining			
				M6 Insulation and vapour barriers are measured in this Section where they are an integral part of the ceiling and are fixed in the ceiling			
3 Isolated strips of suspended ceiling, thickness of lining stated	1 Width ≤ 300 mm 2 and thereafter in 300 mm stages		m	M7 Isolated strips of ceilings are not measured separately between the boundary of the lining and the first line of integral fittings	D3 Isolated strips of ceiling are those which are narrower than the specified relevant lining unit dimension		
4 Items extra over the lining in which they occur	1 Access panels	1 Dimensioned description	nr			C4 Access panels are deemed to include edge trim and fixings	S10 Composition of panels and method of fixing
5 Upstands	1 Thickness of lining	1 Height ≤ 300 mm 2 and thereafter in 300 mm stages	m				S11 Method of support and depth of suspension

CLASSIFICATION TABLE

Classification			Unit	MEASUREMENT RULES	DEFINITION RULES	COVERAGE RULES	SUPPLEMENTARY INFORMATION
6 Irregular window and dormer cheeks	1 Dimensioned description		nr			C5 Irregular window and dormer cheeks are deemed to include cutting and extra supports	
7 Cavity fire barriers, total thickness stated	1 Plain 2 Obstructed by services	1 Height ≤ 300 mm 2 and thereafter in 300 mm stages	m			C6 Cavity fire barriers are deemed to include all scribing, angles, ends, and support work	
8 Edge trims	1 Plain 2 Floating	1 Dimensioned description	m	M8 Trims at regular intervals within the area of suspended ceiling are included within the item description of same 1–3.*.*.5 M9 Trims are measured to openings formed for fittings	D4 Plain edge trims are those which are fixed to the structure D5 Floating edge trims are those which are fixed to the ceiling system	C7 Trims are deemed to include mitred, regular and irregular angles	S12 Centres of fixing
9 Angle trims			m				
10 Items extra over the trims in which they occur	1 Irregular angle pieces		nr		D6 Irregular angle pieces are purpose made manufactured corner pieces		
11 Collars to services passing through fire barriers	1 Pipes 2 Trunking	1 Length of sleeve each side of barrier stated	nr	M10 Collars are measured where they are integral with fire barriers			S13 Types
12 Bridging	1 Span stated	1 Support to light fittings or the like	m	M11 Bridging is measured where widths of trunking in the ceiling space obstruct the standard grid		C8 Bridging is deemed to include additional fixings	
13 Fittings	1 Dimensioned description		nr				

K41 Raised access floors

P1 The following information is shown either on location drawings under A Preliminaries/General conditions or on further drawings which accompany the bills of quantities:
(a) the scope and location of the work

CLASSIFICATION TABLE

				MEASUREMENT RULES	DEFINITION RULES	COVERAGE RULES	SUPPLEMENTARY INFORMATION
1 Floors	1 Thickness of panel stated	1 Height of cavity stated	1 Patterned, details stated	m²			C1 Raised access floors are deemed to include	S1 Kind and quality of materials
					M1 No deduction is made for voids ≤ 0.50 m²		(a) panels, supporting structures, adhesives, bearing pads and the like	S2 Supporting systems
2 Ramps	1 Thickness, length and width stated			nr	M2 The height stated for ramps is the height at each end		(b) cutting and notching and extra supports	S3 Frames to panels
3 Items extra over the floors in which they occur	1 Special panels	1 Dimensioned description		nr				S4 Method of fixing
4 Skirtings and perimeter edge trims	1 Dimensioned description			m	M3 Skirtings and perimeter edge trims not executed as part of the access floor are measured in Section P20		C2 Skirtings and perimeter edge trims are deemed to include ends and angles	

L Windows/Doors/Stairs

L10 Timber windows/rooflights/screens/louvres
L11 Metal windows/rooflights/screens/louvres
L12 Plastics windows/rooflights/screens/louvres

INFORMATION PROVIDED	CLASSIFICATION TABLE		MEASUREMENT RULES	DEFINITION RULES	COVERAGE RULES	SUPPLEMENTARY INFORMATION
P1 Information is shown on location drawings under A Preliminaries/General conditions						
	CLASSIFICATION TABLE					
	1 Windows and window frames	1 Dimensioned diagram nr	M1 Standard sections are identified	D1 All sizes of timber are nominal sizes unless stated as finished sizes	C1 The work is deemed to include notching around obstructions	S1 Kind and quality of materials and if timber whether sawn or wrot
	2 Window shutters	m			C2 Items include:	S2 Preservatives treatment applied as part of the production process
	3 Sun shields				(a) doors where supplied with the unit	S3 Surface treatments applied as part of the production process
	4 Rooflights, skylights, roof windows and frames				(b) architraves, trims, sills, subframes, and the like where part of the component	S4 Selection and protection for subsequent treatment
	5 Screens, borrowed lights and frames				(c) ironmongery where supplied with the component	S5 Matching grain or colour
	6 Shopfronts				(d) finishes where part of the component as delivered	S6 Limits on planing margins on timber and if deviation from stated size is not permitted
	7 Louvres and frames				(e) glazing where supplied with the component	S7 Method of jointing or form of construction
	8 Bedding frames				(f) mechanical operation and automatic operating equipment where supplied with the component	S8 Method of fixing where not at the discretion of the Contractor
	9 Pointing frames				(g) fixings and fastenings	S9 Fixing through vulnerable materials
	10 Bedding and pointing frames					S10 Bedding, jointing and pointing compound

L20 Timber doors/shutters/hatches
L21 Metal doors/shutters/hatches
L22 Plastics/Rubber doors/shutters/hatches

INFORMATION PROVIDED

P1 Information is shown on location drawings under A Preliminaries/General conditions

CLASSIFICATION TABLE

Classification				MEASUREMENT RULES	DEFINITION RULES	COVERAGE RULES	SUPPLEMENTARY INFORMATION
1 Doors 2 Rolling shutters and collapsible gates 3 Sliding/folding partitions 4 Hatches 5 Strong room doors 6 Grilles	1 Dimensioned diagram	nr	1 Approximate weight stated	M1 Standard sections are identified M2 Each leaf of a multi-leafed door is counted as one door M3 Approximate weight is only stated for metal doors and includes their associated frames M4 Doors where supplied with their associated frames or linings are measured as composite items under General rule 9.1 M5 Enumerated composite door frame and lining sets need not state the number of sets within the description	D1 All sizes of timber are nominal sizes unless stated as finished sizes	C1 Doors are deemed to include fitting and hanging whether sawn or wrot C2 The work is deemed to include notching around obstructions C3 Items include: (a) doors where supplied with the unit (b) architraves, trims and the like where part of the component (c) ironmongery where supplied with the component (d) finishes where part of the component (e) glazing where supplied with the component (f) mechanical operation and automatic operating equipment where supplied with the component (g) fixings and fastenings	S1 Kind and quality of materials and if timber whether sawn or wrot S2 Preservatives treatment applied as part of the production process S3 Surface treatments applied as part of the production process S4 Selection and protection for subsequent treatment S5 Matching grain or colour S6 Limits on planing margins on timber and if deviation from stated size is not permitted S7 Method of jointing or form of construction S8 Method of fixing where not at the discretion of the Contractor S9 Fixing through vulnerable materials S10 Bedding, jointing and pointing compound
7 Door frames and door linings, sets (nr) 1 Jambs 2 Heads 3 Sills (nr) 4 Mullions (nr) 5 Transoms (nr)	1 Dimensioned overall cross-section description	m	1 Repeats of identical sets (nr) 2 Different cross-section shapes (nr) 3 Stopped labours (nr)				
6 Composite sets	1 Dimensioned description	nr					
8 Bedding frames 9 Pointing frames 10 Bedding and pointing frames		m					

INFORMATION PROVIDED

P1 Information is shown on location drawings under A Preliminaries/General conditions

CLASSIFICATION TABLE

			Unit
1 Composite item, type stated	1 Dimensioned description		nr
	2 Component drawing		
2 Isolated balustrades	1 Ramps		m
3 Associated handrails	2 Wreaths		
	3 Bends		
	4 Ornamental ends		
	5 Opening portions, details stated		
4 Extra over the isolated balustrades or associated handrails in which they occur	1 Curved, radii stated		nr

MEASUREMENT RULES

M1 Where accessories such as linings, trim nosings, ironmongery etc. are not included in a catalogue reference they are measured in the appropriate Work Sections

M2 Isolated handrails are measured in Section P20

DEFINITION RULES

D1 Work in this Section covers:
(a) staircases, ladders and loft ladders
(b) landings, catwalks and access walkways
(c) balustrades and handrails
(d) hatch doors where part of a loft ladder component

D2 Isolated balustrades are those which do not form an integral part of a staircase unit

D3 Associated handrails are handrails of a material different from the balustrade with which they are associated

COVERAGE RULES

C1 Composite items are deemed to include:
(a) linings, nosings, cover moulds, trims and the like where part of the component
(b) soffit lining, spandrel panels and the like where part of the component
(c) ironmongery and operating gear to loft ladders where supplied with the component
(d) finishes where part of the component as delivered
(e) fixings, fastenings, blockings, wedges, bolts, brackets, cleats and the like

C2 Staircases are deemed to include newels

C3 Plain ends are deemed to be included

SUPPLEMENTARY INFORMATION

S1 Kind and quality of materials and if timber whether sawn or wrot

S2 Preservative treatments applied as part of the production process

S3 Surface treatments applied as part of the production process

S4 Selection and protection for subsequent treatment

S5 Matching grain or colour

S6 Limits on planing margins on timber and if deviation from stated size is not permitted

S7 Method of jointing or form of construction

S8 Method of fixing where not at the discretion of the Contractor

S9 Fixing through vulnerable materials

INFORMATION PROVIDED

P1 Information is shown on location drawings under A Preliminaries/General conditions

			MEASUREMENT RULES	DEFINITION RULES	COVERAGE RULES	SUPPLEMENTARY INFORMATION
			M1 Each pane is measured separately for multiple glazed panes where not in sealed units	D1 Multiple glazed panes are the constituent panes of glazing of more than one layer	C1 Glazing is deemed to include raking and curved cutting	S1 Kind, quality and thickness of glass
						S2 Kind and quality of glazing compound – where more than single compound refer to 11.0.0.0
			M2 Labours on edges of glass louvre panes are given in the description			S3 Method of glazing
						S4 Method of securing including details of gaskets where gasket glazed
						S5 Nature of frame or surround

CLASSIFICATION TABLE

1 Standard plain glass				MEASUREMENT RULES	DEFINITION RULES	COVERAGE RULES	SUPPLEMENTARY INFORMATION
	1 Glazing	1 Panes (nr), area ≤ 0.15 m²	m²	1 ≥ 50 identical panes (nr), size stated	D2 Standard plain glass is any glass (other than a special glass) which is ≤ 10 mm thick and in panes ≤ 4 m² and is not drilled, not brilliant cut and not bent		
		2 Panes, area 0.15 – 4.00 m²		2 Irregular shaped panes			
				3 Multiple glazed panes			
				4 Glazing rebates 20 – 30 mm			
				5 and thereafter in 10 mm stages			
	2 Louvres	1 Dimensioned description	nr	6 Panes required to align with adjacent panes			

CLASSIFICATION TABLE				Unit		MEASUREMENT RULES	DEFINITION RULES	COVERAGE RULES	SUPPLEMENTARY INFORMATION
2 Non-standard plain glass	1 Glazing 2 Louvres	1 Dimensioned description		nr	1 Multiple glazed panes 2 Glazing rebates 20–30 mm 3 and thereafter in 10 mm stages 4 Brilliant cut panes, type of decoration stated 5 Bent in long dimension, radii stated 6 Bent in short dimension, radii stated 7 Bent in both dimensions, radii stated 8 Drilled panes, diameter, size and type of holes (nr) stated 9 Drilled panes with insulating sleeves, diameter, size and type of holes (nr) stated 10 Panes required to align with adjacent panes		D3 Non-standard plain glass is any glass (other than special glass) which is > 10 mm thick or is in panes > 4 m² or is drilled, brilliant cut or bent		
3 Special glass	1 Glazing 2 Louvres	1 Dimensioned description		nr			D4 Special glass includes: (a) laminated (b) toughened (c) enamelled and toughened (d) bullet resistant (e) anti-bandit (f) solar control (g) sealed double glazing units (h) sealed multiple glazing units (j) lead (k) acrylic (l) polycarbonate (m) bullions		
4 Glass shop fronts	1 Component drawing reference			nr		M4 Glass shop fronts involving simple glass joints and glass reinforcing fins are measured here. Suspended glass shop fronts are measured in Section H13	D5 The component drawing referred to is to include details of the stiffeners		
5 Polished edges 6 Bevelled edges, width of bevel stated	1 Edges			m	1 Curved edges 2 Bent panes	M5 Labours on glass are grouped with the glass to which they relate		C2 Polished and bevelled edges are deemed to include external mitres	S6 Type and method of forming edges and shapings
	2 Internal mitres 3 Scallops and other shapings, details stated			nr					
7 Grinding 8 Sandblasting 9 Embossing 10 Engraving	1 Plain work			m²	1 Panes partly obscured 2 Panes wholly obscured	M6 Grinding, sandblasting and embossing are measured over the whole area of the pane			S7 Type of acid work for embossing
	2 Design work	1 Dimensioned description		nr	1 One or more dimensions ≤ 300 mm, size of pane stated				
11 Strips or channels for edges of panes				m	1 Fixed with other materials, type stated				S8 Kind, quality and size of materials

12 Mirrors	1 Dimensioned description	nr		M7 Mirrors fixed to walls or glazed into openings are measured here. Small mirrors in toilets, dressing rooms and the like are measured in Section N10	S9 Details of protective backings S10 Method of fixing S11 Fixing through vulnerable materials
13 Hacking out existing glass and preparing rebates	1 Type of sash or other surround and method of glazing stated together with type of glass	m	1 Beads for re-use, details stated	M8 Hacking out existing glass and preparing rebates is measured the perimeter of the pane	

L41 Lead light glazing

INFORMATION PROVIDED

P1 Information is shown on location drawings under A Preliminaries/General conditions

CLASSIFICATION TABLE

					MEASUREMENT RULES	DEFINITION RULES	COVERAGE RULES	SUPPLEMENTARY INFORMATION
1 Lead light glazing	1 Both dimensions of lights > 300 mm	1 Shape and average size of panes stated	m²	1 Panes required to align with adjacent panes	M1 The requirement to state the average size of panes is related to each light			S1 Kind, quality and thickness of glass
	2 One dimension only of lights ≤ 300 mm		m					S2 Kind and quality of glazing compound
	3 Both dimensions of lights ≤ 300 mm		nr					S3 Method of glazing
2 Saddle bars	1 Length > 300 mm		m					S4 Nature of frame or surround
	2 Length ≤ 300 mm		nr					S5 Type, section and nominal or finished width of cames and details of reinforcement

INFORMATION PROVIDED

P1 Information is shown on location drawings under A Preliminaries/General conditions

CLASSIFICATION TABLE

		MEASUREMENT RULES	DEFINITION RULES	COVERAGE RULES	SUPPLEMENTARY INFORMATION
1 Infill panels (nr)	1 Curved, radii stated 2 Panels, exceeding size of normal manufactured unit 3 Panels requiring special treatment to edges m²	D1 Work is deemed to be internal unless described as external D2 Infill panels are non-glass and non-glass plastics rigid sheet spandrel and infill panels of all kinds fixed with beads, gaskets and the like into wood, metal, plastics and concrete surrounds excluding panels/sheets forming an integral part of a component or proprietary cladding system	C1 Infill panels are deemed to include glazing compounds, sealants, intumescent mastic, distance pieces, location and setting blocks, and fixings	S1 Kind and quality of materials and if timber whether sawn or wrot S2 Preservative treatments applied as part of the production process S3 Surface treatments applied as part of the production process S4 Selection and protection for subsequent treatment S5 Matching grain or colour S6 Limits on planing margins on timber and if deviation from stated size is not permitted S7 Form of construction and jointing details where individual panel in more than one piece S8 Thickness or substance S9 Method of fixing where not at the discretion of the Contractor S10 Restrictions on cutting panels and treatment of edges

M Surface finishes

M10 Sand cement/Concrete/Granolithic screeds/flooring
M12 Trowelled bitumen/resin/rubber-latex flooring
M20 Plastered/Rendered/Roughcast coatings
M23 Resin bound mineral coatings
J10 Specialist waterproof rendering

INFORMATION PROVIDED

P1 The following information is shown either on location drawings under A Preliminaries/General conditions or on further drawings which accompany the bills of quantities:

(a) the scope and location of the work

CLASSIFICATION TABLE

1 Walls	1 Width > 300 mm	1 Thickness and number of coats stated	m²	1 Patterned, details stated
2 Ceilings	2 Width ≤ 300 mm	2 Thickness of plasterboard or other rigid sheet lathing and thickness and number of coats stated	m	2 Floors laid in bays, average size of bays stated
3 Isolated beams				3 Floors laid in one operation with their base stated
4 Isolated columns				4 Overhand work

MEASUREMENT RULES	DEFINITION RULES	COVERAGE RULES	SUPPLEMENTARY INFORMATION
M1 Resinous floor/wall finishes applied by brush or roller are measured in Section M60	D1 The work is deemed internal unless described as external	C1 The work is deemed to include: (a) fair joints (b) outlets, working over and around obstructions, pipes and the like, into recesses and shaped inserts (c) bonding agents where included with the work	S1 Kind, quality, composition and mix of materials including waterproofing agents and other admixtures and plasterboard or other rigid sheet lathing
M2 The area measured is that in contact with the base and no deduction is made for voids ≤ 0.50 m² or grounds	D2 The thickness stated is the nominal thickness		S2 Method of application
M3 Work in staircase areas and plant rooms are each given separately	D3 Rounded internal and external angles > 100 mm radius are classified as curved work	C2 Patterned work is deemed to include all extra work involved	S3 Nature of surface treatment including wax polishing or resin sealing coat
M4 Work to ceilings and beams over 3.50 m above floor (measured to ceiling level in both cases), except in staircase areas, is so described stating the height in further 1.50 m stages	D4 Floors include landings		S4 Special curing of finished work
M5 Curved work is so described with the radii stated measured on face	D5 Work to sides and soffits of attached beams and openings and to sides of attached columns is classified as work to the abutting walls or ceilings	C3 Plasterboard or other sheet backing is deemed to include joint reinforcing scrim	S5 Nature of base
M6 Width is the width of each face	D6 Beams and columns are classified as isolated where the work is different from the abutting ceilings or walls	C4 Work to walls, ceilings, beams and columns is deemed to include internal and external angles and intersections ≤ 10 mm radius	S6 Preparatory work where bonding is included with the work
			S7 Details of work to be carried out prior to fixing of frames or linings
			S8 Method of fixing and jointing plasterboard or other rigid sheet lathing

Item	Classification	Dimensions stated	Unit	Supplementary information	Rules
5 Floors 6 Roofs	1 Level and to falls only ≤ 15° from horizontal 2 To falls and crossfalls and to slopes ≤ 15° from horizontal 3 To slopes > 15° from horizontal		m²		C5 Work to floors and roofs is deemed to include: (a) forming shallow channels within the thickness of the screed or flooring (b) intersections in sloping work
7 Treads		1 Width and thickness stated	m	1 Patterned, details stated 2 Inserts, size or section stated 3 Moulded, shape stated	C6 Treads and risers are deemed to include fair edges, internal and external angles and intersections ≤ 10 mm radius
8 Risers	1 Plain 2 Undercut	1 Height and thickness stated 2 Dimensioned description	m		
9 Strings 10 Aprons		1 Width and thickness stated 2 Dimensioned description 3 Moulded, shape stated	m		C7 Strings and aprons are deemed to include ends, angles, ramped and wreathed corners and intersections ≤ 10 mm radius
11 Margins		1 Width and thickness stated	m		C8 Margins are deemed to include fair edges and flush joints
12 Linings to channels	1 Girth on face stated	1 Horizontal 2 To falls	m		C9 Linings to channels are deemed to include arrises, coves, ends, angles and intersections and outlets
13 Skirtings 14 Kerbs 15 Cappings		1 Height or width or girth and thickness stated 2 Dimensioned description	m	1 Patterned, details stated 2 Flush 3 Raking 4 Vertical 5 Inserts, size or section stated 6 Moulded, shape stated	C10 Skirtings, kerbs and cappings are deemed to include fair edges, rounded edges, beaded edges, coved junctions, ends, angles and ramps
16 Rounded angles and intersections			m	M7 Rounded angles and intersections are only measured in the range 10–100 mm radius	

CLASSIFICATION TABLE

Classification				Unit
17 Coves		1 Girth stated	1 Patterned, details stated	m
18 Mouldings		2 Dimensioned description	2 Raking	
19 Cornices			3 Vertical	
20 Architraves			4 Enrichments	
21 Ceiling ribs			5 Undercut	
22 Bands	1 Flush		6 Bracketing	
	2 Raised		7 Flat tops	
	3 Sunk		8 Weathered tops	
23 Items extra over the work in which they occur	1 Ends	1 Details stated		nr
	2 Internal angles			
	3 External angles			
	4 Intersections			
24 Accessories	1 Reinforcement, details stated	1 Walls		m²
	2 Board insulation, thickness stated	2 Ceilings		
	3 Quilt insulation, thickness stated	3 Isolated beams		
	4 Separating membranes, thickness stated	4 Isolated columns		
	5 Movement joints	5 Floors	1 Dimensioned description	m
	6 Cover strips	6 Roofs		
	7 Dividing strip			
	8 Beads, function stated			
	9 Nosings			
	10 Anti-crack strips ≤ 300 mm wide			
25 Precast plaster components	1 Dimensioned description			nr
26 Temporary support work to the face of risers and the like	1 Height stated	1 Undercut		m

MEASUREMENT RULES

M8 Coves, mouldings, cornices, architraves, ceiling ribs and bands are measured the length in contact with the base

M9 Measured extra over 17 – 22.0.*.*

DEFINITION RULES

D7 Movement joints include expansion joints

D8 Function of beads as angle beads, casing beads, and the like are stated

D9 Components include vent grilles and ornaments

COVERAGE RULES

C11 Beads and nosings are deemed to include working finishings thereto

SUPPLEMENTARY INFORMATION

S9 Method of fixing where not at the discretion of the Contractor

INFORMATION PROVIDED

P1 The following information is shown either on location drawings under A Preliminaries/General conditions or on further drawings which accompany the bills of quantities:
(a) the scope and location of the work

CLASSIFICATION TABLE

				MEASUREMENT RULES	DEFINITION RULES	COVERAGE RULES	SUPPLEMENTARY INFORMATION
				M1 Only proprietary construction is measured in this Section	D1 The work is deemed external unless otherwise described as internal	C1 Work is deemed to include:	S1 Proprietary name, kind, quality and thickness of board insulation and method of fixing
				M2 Curved work is so described with the radii stated measured on face	D2 Rounded internal and external angles > 100 mm are classified as curved work	(a) fair joints	S2 Construction of metal lathing
						(b) working over and around obstructions into recesses and shaped inserts	S3 Kind, quality, composition, mix, and method of application and of materials for rendering
						(c) internal and external angles and intersections	S4 Type of adhesive renders with glass fibre matting
						(d) joint and reinforcing tape	S5 Nature of surface finish
						(e) plaster dabs	S6 Nature of base
							S7 Details of preparatory work where bonding is included with the work
1 Walls	1 Width > 300 mm	1 Total thickness and number of coats of rendering stated	m²			C2 The work is deemed to include accessories for fixing	
2 Ceilings			1 Overhand work				
3 Isolated beams	2 Width ≤ 300 mm		m		M3 The area measured is that in contact with the base and no deduction is made for voids ≤ 0.50 m²	D3 The thickness stated is the nominal thickness	
					M4 Width is the width on face	D4 Work to sides and soffits of openings is regarded as work to the abutting walls	
4 Beads, function stated	1 Dimensioned description		m			D5 Function of beads as angle beads, casing beads, and the like are stated	C3 Beads, nosings and expansion strips are deemed to include working finishings thereto
5 Nosings							
6 Expansion strips							

INFORMATION PROVIDED

P1 The following information is shown either on location drawings under A Preliminaries/General conditions or on further drawings which accompany the bills of quantities:

(a) the scope and location of the work

CLASSIFICATION TABLE

			MEASUREMENT RULES	DEFINITION RULES	COVERAGE RULES	SUPPLEMENTARY INFORMATION
1 Walls and columns 2 Ceilings and Beams 3 Structural metalwork	1 Thickness and number of coats stated	m²	M1 The area measured is that in contact with the base and no deduction is made for voids ≤ 0.50 m² or grounds M2 Work in staircase areas and plant rooms are each given separately M3 Work to ceilings and beams over 3.50 m above floor (measured to ceiling level in both cases), except in staircase areas, is so described stating the height in further 1.50 m stages	D1 The work is deemed as internal unless described as external	C1 Work is deemed to include: (a) fair joints (b) additional labour for overhand work (c) angles, intersections and curved work	S1 Kind and quantity of materials including plasterboard or other rigid sheet lathing S2 Nature of base S3 Preparatory work including bonding agents S4 Priming or sealing coats S5 Surface finish S6 Method of application S7 Method of fixing where not at the discretion of the Contractor
	2 Thickness of plasterboard or other rigid sheet lathing and thickness and number of coats stated					
4 Accessories	1 Beads, function stated 2 Nosings 3 Anti-crack strips ≤ 300 mm wide	m		D2 Function of beads as angle beads, casing beads, and the like are stated	C2 Beads and nosings are deemed to include working finishings thereto	

INFORMATION PROVIDED

P1 The following information is shown either on location drawings under A Preliminaries/General conditions or on further drawings which accompany the bills of quantities:

(a) the scope and location of the work

(b) the services located within the lathing, where the work includes complex integral services

CLASSIFICATION TABLE

			MEASUREMENT RULES	DEFINITION RULES	COVERAGE RULES	SUPPLEMENTARY INFORMATION
1 Suspended lathing ceilings	1 Depth of suspension ≤ 150 mm 2 Depth of suspension 150 – 500 mm 3 and thereafter in 500 mm stages	1 Method of fixing suspension system to structure	m²	M1 Work in staircase areas and plant rooms are each given separately M2 Work to ceilings and beams over 3.50 m above floor (measured to ceiling level in both cases), except in staircase areas, is so described stating the height in further 1.50 m stages M3 Curved work is so described with the radii stated measured on face M4 The area measured is that between boundaries and soffits of attached beams and openings and to sides of attached columns is measured as work to the abutting walls or ceilings	D1 All work is deemed internal unless described as external D2 Rounded internal and external angles > 100 mm radius are classified as curved work D3 Lathing to sides and soffits of attached beams and openings and to sides of attached columns is measured as work to the abutting walls or ceilings D4 Lathing to ceilings includes lathing to sloping ceilings	C1 Work is deemed to include: (a) mechanical fixings to solid backings, steel rods, stirrups, spacer rods and hangers (b) steel channel framing (c) screws, staples, clips, clout nails, wire ties, steel banding, and other fixings (d) additional support and trimming for light fittings (e) internal and external angles < 100 mm radius	S1 Kind and quality of materials S2 Construction of framing and suspension system S3 Extent of laps and method of jointing
2 Walls	1 Width > 300 mm 2 Width ≤ 300 mm	1 Method of fixing to structure	m²				
3 Ceilings							
4 Isolated beams				M5 Width is the width of each face			
5 Isolated columns							
6 Upstands	1 Height ≤ 300 mm 2 and thereafter in 300 mm stages	1 Method of fixing suspension system to structure	m				
7 Bridging	1 Span stated	1 Supports to light fittings and the like	m	M6 Bridging is measured where the width of trunking or the like in the ceiling space obstructs the standard grid		C2 Bridging is deemed to include additional fixings	
8 Irregular window and dormer cheeks	1 Dimensioned description		nr	1 Suspension system obstructed by services		C3 Irregular window and cheeks are deemed to include cutting and extra supports.	

INFORMATION PROVIDED

P1 The following information is shown either on location drawings under A Preliminaries/General conditions or on further drawings which accompany the bills of quantities:
(a) the scope and location of the work

CLASSIFICATION TABLE

			Unit		MEASUREMENT RULES	DEFINITION RULES	COVERAGE RULES	SUPPLEMENTARY INFORMATION
1 Walls 2 Ceilings	1 Width > 300 mm	1 Thickness stated	m²	1 Plain slab 2 Panelled slab 3 Patterned, details stated	M1 Area measured is that in contact with the base and no deduction is made for voids ≤ 0.50 m² or grounds	D1 All work is deemed internal unless described as external	C1 Fibrous plaster is deemed to include: (a) fair joints (b) reinforcement (c) canvas (d) moulds (e) screws and other fixings	S1 Kind, quality, composition and mix of materials S2 Method of fixing and treatment of joints S3 Nature of base S4 Timber or metal lathing and reinforcement
	2 Width ≤ 300 mm		m		M2 Work in staircase areas and plant rooms are each given separately			
3 Items extra over the fibrous plaster in which they occur	1 Access panels	1 Dimensioned description	nr		M3 Work to ceilings and beams over 3.50 m above floor (measured to ceiling level in both cases), except in staircase areas, is so described stating the height in further 1.50 m stages		C2 Access panels are deemed to include cutting around edges and providing extra materials	
4 Arches 5 Domes 6 Groined soffits					M4 Curved work is so described stating the radii stated measured on face			
7 Plain casings	1 Beams 2 Columns 3 Stanchions	1 Girth stated	m		M5 Width is the width of each face	D2 Plain casings to piers and pilasters are classified as to columns		
8 Moulded casings 9 Ornamental casings		1 Dimensioned description	nr	1 Patterned, details stated 2 Shaft caps 3 Bases				

Item			Unit		Notes
10 Coves				1 Patterned, details stated	
11 Mouldings				2 Raking	M6 The lengths measured for coves, mouldings, cornices and architraves are their extreme lengths
12 Cornices			m	3 Vertical	
13 Architraves				4 Enrichments	
				5 Undercut	
14 Items extra over the work in which they occur	1 Ends 2 Internal angles 3 External angles 4 Intersections	1 Details stated	nr		M7 Measured extra over 10 – 13.0.1.*
15 Ornaments	1 Character stated	1 Character stated	nr		D3 Ornaments are irregularly occurring features
16 Consoles					
17 Overdoors		1 Character stated			
18 Canopies					
19 Fireplace surrounds					
20 Specially made models		1 Dimensioned description	nr	1 Temporarily fixed in the building for inspection 2 Modeller's grounds, details stated 3 Modeller's boards, details stated	
21 Full size cartoons					

INFORMATION PROVIDED

P1 The following information is shown either on location drawings under A Preliminaries/General conditions or on further drawings which accompany the bills of quantities:
(a) the scope and location of the work

CLASSIFICATION TABLE

Classification	Sub-classification	Unit
1 Walls 2 Ceilings 3 Isolated beams	1 Plain, width > 300 mm	m²
	2 Plain, width ≤ 300 mm	m
	3 Work with joints laid out to detail, width > 300 mm	m²
	4 Work with joints laid out to detail, width ≤ 300 mm	m
4 Isolated columns	1 Dimensioned description	
	1 Patterned, details stated 2 Tiles with long side horizontal	
5 Floors	1 Level or to falls only ≤ 15° from horizontal 2 To falls and crossfalls and to slopes ≤ 15° from horizontal 3 To slopes > 15° from horizontal	
	1 Plain 2 Work with joints laid out to detail, dimensioned diagram stated	m²
	1 Patterned work, details stated 2 Floors laid in bays, average size of bays stated 3 Inserts, size or section stated	

MEASUREMENT RULES

M1 Work is measured on the exposed face and no deduction is made for voids ≤ 0.50 m²

M2 Work in staircase areas and plant rooms are each given separately

M3 Work to ceilings and beams over 3.50 m above floor (measured to ceiling level in both cases), except in staircase areas, is so described stating the height in further 1.50 m stages

M4 Curved work is so described stating the radii stated measured on face

M5 Width is the width of each face

DEFINITION RULES

D1 All work is deemed internal unless described as external

D2 The thickness stated is the thickness exclusive of keys, grooves and the like

D3 Rounded internal and external angles > 10 mm radius are classified as curved work where not measured under 15.1–3.1.0

D4 Beams and columns are classified as isolated where the work is different from the abutting ceilings or walls

D5 Work to sides and soffits of attached beams and openings and to sides of attached columns is classed as work to the abutting walls or ceilings

D6 Tiles are deemed to be laid with their long side vertical unless otherwise described

D7 Floors include landings

COVERAGE RULES

C1 The work is deemed to include:
(a) fair joints
(b) working over and around obstructions
(c) additional labour for overhand work
(d) cutting
(e) drainage holes
(f) bedding mortars and adhesives
(g) grouting
(h) cleaning, sealing and polishing

C2 Work to walls, ceilings, beams and columns is deemed to include internal and external angles and intersections ≤ 10 mm radius

C3 Work to floors is deemed to include intersections in sloping work

SUPPLEMENTARY INFORMATION

S1 Kind and quality of materials
S2 Size, shape and thickness of units
S3 Nature of base
S4 Preparatory work
S5 Nature of finished surface including any sealing/polishing
S6 Bedding or other method of fixing
S7 Treatment of joints
S8 Layout of joints

	First division	Second division	Third division	Unit	Supplementary
6 Treads		1 Width stated		m	
7 Sills					
8 Risers	1 Plain 2 Undercut	1 Height stated		m	1 Undercut
9 Strings					
10 Aprons		1 Height stated		m	
11 Linings to channels	1 Horizontal 2 To falls	1 Girth on face stated		m	1 Patterned work, details stated 2 Inserts, size or section stated 3 Flush 4 Raking 5 Vertical
12 Skirtings					
13 Kerbs	1 Height stated 2 Height and width stated			m	
14 Corner pieces	1 Dimensioned description			nr	
15 Items extra over the work in which they occur	1 Special tiles 2 Special slabs 3 Special blocks	1 Dimensioned description		m	
	4 Access units 5 Isolated special units	2 Manufacturer's reference		nr	
16 Accessories	1 Separating membranes, thickness stated		1 Dimensioned description	m²	
	2 Movement joints	1 Dimensioned description		m	1 In situ 2 Precast
	3 Cover strips 4 Dividing strips				
	5 Ornaments, dimensioned description and character stated			nr	

C4 Work to treads, sills and risers is deemed to include fair edges, internal and external angles

C5 Curved treads, risers, strings and aprons are deemed to include curved and radiused cutting for special edge tiles

C6 Strings and aprons are deemed to include fair edges, ends, angles and ramps

C7 Linings to channels are deemed to include arrises, coves, ends, angles, intersections and outlets

C8 Skirtings and kerbs are deemed to include fair edges, rounded edges, ends, angles and ramps

D8 Special tiles include non-standard tiles to produce fair edges, internal and external angles, moulded edges, beaded edges, and coved junctions

D9 Movement joints include expansion joints

D10 Ornaments are irregularly occurring features

S9 Method of fixing

INFORMATION PROVIDED

P1 The following information is shown either on location drawings under A Preliminaries/General conditions or on further drawings which accompany the bills of quantities:

(a) the scope and location of the work

CLASSIFICATION TABLE

			MEASUREMENT RULES	DEFINITION RULES	COVERAGE RULES	SUPPLEMENTARY INFORMATION
1 Terrazzo tiling			M1 Terrazzo tiling is measured in accordance with the rules for Section M40			
2 In situ terrazzo			M2 In situ terrazzo is measured in accordance with the rules for Section M10			

M50 Rubber/Plastics/Cork/Lino/Carpet tiling/sheeting
M51 Edge fixed carpeting

INFORMATION PROVIDED

P1 The following information is shown either on location drawings under A Preliminaries/General conditions or on further drawings which accompany the bills of quantities:

(a) the scope and location of the work

CLASSIFICATION TABLE

	MEASUREMENT RULES	DEFINITION RULES	COVERAGE RULES	SUPPLEMENTARY INFORMATION
	M1 Area measured is that in contact with the base and no deduction is made for voids ≤ 0.50 m²	D1 The work is deemed internal unless described as external	C1 The work is deemed to include:	S1 Kind, quality and size of materials
	M2 Work in staircase areas and plant rooms are each given separately	D2 Rounded internal and external angles > 100 mm radius are classified as curved work	(a) fair joints	S2 Nature and number of underlays
	M3 Work to ceilings and beams over 3.50 m above floor (measured to ceiling level in both cases), except in staircase areas, is so described stating the height in further 1.50 m stages		(b) working over and around obstructions, into recesses and shaped inserts	S3 Extent of laps
	M4 Curved work is so described with the radii stated measured on face		(c) additional labour for overhand work	S4 Type of seams
			(d) fixing at perimeter	S5 Nature of base
				S6 Surface treatment
				S7 Pattern, width and laying direction of materials
				S8 Method of fixing and treatment of joints

	First	Second	Third	Unit	Fourth
1	Walls		1 Method of fixing and treatment of joints stated	m²	1 Patterned, details stated
2	Ceilings				2 Inserts, size or section stated
3	Isolated beams				3 Underlays
4	Isolated columns				
5	Floors	1 Width > 300 mm	1 Level or to falls only ≤ 15° from horizontal	m²	
			2 To falls and crossfalls ≤ 15° from horizontal		
			3 To slopes > 15° from horizontal		
		2 Width ≤ 300 mm		m	
6	Strings	1 Width stated	1 Height stated	m	1 Patterned, details stated
7	Aprons				2 Inserts, size or section stated
8	Treads			m	
9	Risers	1 Plain	1 Height stated	m	
		2 Undercut			
10	Skirtings		1 Height stated	m	1 Patterned, details stated
11	Kerbs		2 Height and width stated		2 Inserts, size or section stated
					3 Flush
					4 Raking
					5 Vertical
12	Lining to channels		1 Girth on face stated	m	1 Patterned, details stated
					2 Inserts, size or section stated
13	Accessories	1 Separating membranes, thickness stated		m²	
		2 Nosings	1 Dimensioned description	m	
		3 Movement joints		m	
		4 Cover strips			
		5 Dividing strips			
		6 Stair rods		nr	
		7 Carpet holders			
		8 Carpet clips or grippers			
		9 Binder bars			

M5 Width is the width of each face

M6 Items are only measured separately where they are not fixings at perimeter see C1(d)

D3 Work to sides and soffits of attached beams and openings and to sides of attached columns is classed as work to the abutting walls or ceilings

D4 Beams and columns are classified as isolated where the work is different from the abutting ceilings or walls respectively

D5 Movement joints include expansion joints

C2 The work is deemed to include external angles, rounded internal and external angles ≤ 100 mm radius

C3 Work to sides and soffits of attached beams and openings and to sides of attached columns is classed as work to the abutting walls or ceilings

C4 Work to falls, crossfalls and slopes is deemed to include intersections

C5 Work to strings and aprons is deemed to include ends, angles, ramped and wreathed corners

C6 Work to treads and risers is deemed to include all fair edges, internal and external angles

C7 Work to skirtings and kerbs is deemed to include fair edges, rounded edges, beaded edges, moulded edges, coved junctions, ends, angles and ramps

C8 Linings to channels are deemed to include arrises, coves, ends, angles, intersections and outlets

C9 Nosings are deemed to include working finishings thereto

C10 Mitred regular and irregular angles are deemed included

INFORMATION PROVIDED

P1 Information is shown on location drawings under A Preliminaries/General conditions

CLASSIFICATION TABLE

1 Walls and columns	1 Areas > 0.50 m²		m²	1 Raking and curved cutting
2 Ceilings and beams	2 Areas ≤ 0.50 m²		nr	2 Lining paper
3 Border strips			m	1 Cutting border strips to profile
4 Corners			nr	1 Cutting corners to profile
5 Motifs				2 Cutting motifs to profile

MEASUREMENT RULES

M1 Where the manufacturer and pattern cannot be fully described work is measured as hanging/fixing only and the supply and delivery to site of papers/fabrics is covered by a prime cost or provisional sum

M2 Work in staircase areas is given separately

M3 The areas or lengths measured are the areas or lengths covered including allowances for the extra lengths of edges, mouldings, panels, sinkings, corrugations, flutings, carvings, enrichments and the like

M4 No deduction is made for voids ≤ 0.50 m²

M5 Work to ceilings and beams over 3.50 m above floor (measured to ceiling level in both cases), except in staircase areas, is so described stating the height in further 1.50 m stages

DEFINITION RULES

D1 Paper is deemed to be hung vertically unless described otherwise

COVERAGE RULES

C1 The work is deemed to include cutting or fitting around obstructions, intrusions or projections

C2 Border strips are deemed to include mitres and intersections

SUPPLEMENTARY INFORMATION

S1 Kind and quality of materials, manufacturer and pattern

S2 Nature of base

S3 Preparatory work

S4 Method of fixing and jointing

INFORMATION PROVIDED

P1 Information is shown on location drawings under A Preliminaries/General conditions

CLASSIFICATION TABLE

1 General surfaces				MEASUREMENT RULES	DEFINITION RULES	COVERAGE RULES	SUPPLEMENTARY INFORMATION
1 Girth > 300 mm	m²	1 Multi-coloured work		M1 Work in staircase areas and plant rooms are each given separately	D1 Work is deemed to be internal unless otherwise described	C1 The work is deemed to include rubbing down with glass, emery or sand paper	S1 Kind and quality of materials
2 Isolated surfaces, girth ≤ 300 mm	m	2 Features unpainted, details stated		M2 The area or girth measured is the area or girth covered including allowances for the extra girth of edges, mouldings, panels, sinkings, corrugations, flutings, carvings, enrichments and the like unless otherwise provided herein.	D2 Multi-coloured work is defined as the application of more than one colour on an individual surface except on walls and piers or on ceilings and beams	C2 Multi-coloured work is deemed to include cutting in and cutting to line	S2 Nature of base
3 Isolated areas ≤ 0.50 m² irrespective of girth	nr	3 Irregular surfaces			D3 Multi-coloured work on walls and piers or on ceilings and beams shall be defined as the application in one room of more than one colour on either the walls and piers or ceilings and beams		S3 Preparatory work
		4 Application on site prior to fixing		M3 No deduction is made for voids ≤ 0.50 m²	D4 Irregular surfaces are corrugated, fluted, panelled, carved or ornamental surfaces		S4 Priming or sealing coats
				M4 Work to ceilings and beams over 3.50 m above floor (measured to ceiling level in both cases), except in staircase areas, is so described stating the height in further 1.50 m stages	D5 Features unpainted include fire stripping and weather stripping		S5 Undercoats (nr)
					D6 Isolated surfaces include the girth of associated mouldings		S6 Finishing coats (nr) and surface finish
					D7 Where reference within this table is made to painting it is deemed to include clear finishing as applicable		S7 Method of application
					D8 General surfaces are those not included in other Classifications	C3 Work to general surfaces is deemed to include work on butts and fastenings attached to doors, frames and linings	S8 Abrasive or other treatment applied between coats other than rubbing down with glass, emery or sand paper

CLASSIFICATION TABLE

			Unit
2 Glazed windows and screens	1 Panes, area ≤ 0.10 m²		m²
	2 Panes, area 0.10 – 0.50 m²		
	3 Panes, area 0.50 – 1.00 m²		
	4 Panes, area > 1.00 m²		
3 Glazed sash windows			
4 Glazed doors			
5 Structural metalwork	1 General surfaces	1 Girth > 300 mm	m²
		2 Isolated surfaces, girth ≤ 300 mm	m
		3 Isolated areas ≤ 0.50 m² irrespective of girth	nr
	2 Members of roof trusses, lattice girders, purlins and the like	1 Girth > 300 mm	m²
		2 Isolated surfaces, girth ≤ 300 mm	m
		3 Isolated areas ≤ 0.50 m² irrespective of girth	nr
6 Radiators	1 Panel type	1 Girth > 300 mm	m²
	2 Column type	2 Isolated surfaces, girth ≤ 300 mm	m
		3 Isolated areas ≤ 0.50 m² irrespective of girth	nr
7 Railings, fences and gates	1 Plain open type	1 Girth > 300 mm	m²
	2 Close type	2 Isolated surfaces, girth ≤ 300 mm	m
	3 Ornamental type	3 Isolated areas ≤ 0.50 m² irrespective of girth	m²

SUPPLEMENTARY INFORMATION

1 Multi-coloured work
2 Features unpainted, details stated
3 Partially glazed
4 Irregular surfaces
5 Application on site to members prior to fixing

1 Multi-coloured work
2 Features unpainted, details stated
3 Application on site to members prior to fixing
4 Structural metalwork height 5.00 – 8.00 m above floor level
5 and thereafter in 3.0 m stages

MEASUREMENT RULES

M5 The area measured is each side of windows, screens and glazed doors, measured flat plus edges of glazed doors

M6 Where panes of more than one size occur then the sizes are averaged

M7 Work to associated linings and sills are measured as general surfaces

M8 The height of structural metalwork is measured to the highest point of the members in the stated height range

M9 Radiators are measured the area painted

M10 Plain open type fencing and gates are classified according to the size of their individual members

M11 Each side of close type fencing and gates is measured overall

M12 Each side of ornamental railings and gates is measured and notwithstanding the general measurement rule above is measured overall regardless of voids

DEFINITION RULES

D9 Pane areas are those of individual panes

D10 Examples of plain open type fencing are plain post and rail, post and wire, chain link, wire mesh, cleft pale, palisade and metal bar

D11 Examples of close type fencing are close boarded, built up concrete and corrugated

COVERAGE RULES

C4 Glazed work is deemed to include:
(a) edges of opening lights and portions uncovered by sliding sashes in double hung casements
(b) additional painting to the surrounding frame caused by opening lights
(c) cutting in next glass
(d) work on glazing beads, butts and fastenings attached thereto

C5 Work to structural metalwork is deemed to include work to attached hookbolts, clips and the like

C6 Work to radiators is deemed to include work to brackets and stays

				Supplementary information	Rules
8 Gutters	1 Valley and parapet	1 Girth > 300 mm	m²		C7 Work to gutters is deemed to include work to gutter brackets
		2 Isolated surfaces, girth ≤ 300 mm	m		
		3 Isolated areas ≤ 0.50 m² irrespective of girth	nr		
	2 Eaves	1 Girth > 300 mm	m²		
		2 Isolated surfaces, girth ≤ 300 mm	m		
		3 Isolated areas ≤ 0.50 m² irrespective of girth	nr		
9 Services		1 Description stated	m²	1 Multi-coloured work	D12 Services include pipes, lagged pipes, conduits, cables, ducting, trunking, straps, standards, bars and the like
				2 Features unpainted, details stated	D13 Painting to isolated services units such as ventilating gratings, soot-doors, flushing cisterns, rainwater heads, strap hinges and the like is classed as painting services
				3 Painted throughout in coded colours	C8 Work to services is deemed to include work to saddles, pipehooks, holderbats, conduit boxes and other components for fixing
				4 Application on site to members prior to fixing	
10 Coloured bands for coding service pipes	1 Colours (nr)	1 Description stated	nr		

N10 General fixtures/furnishings/equipment
N11 Domestic kitchen fittings
N12 Catering equipment
N13 Sanitary appliances/fittings
N15 Signs/Notices
N20, 21, 22, 23 Special purpose fixtures/furnishings/equipment
Q50 Site/Street furniture/equipment

INFORMATION PROVIDED

P1 Information is shown on location drawings under A Preliminaries/General conditions

CLASSIFICATION TABLE

Classification			Unit	MEASUREMENT RULES	DEFINITION RULES	COVERAGE RULES	SUPPLEMENTARY INFORMATION
1 Fixtures, furnishings and equipment not associated with services	1 Component drawing reference		nr	M1 It is permissible in respect of any individual item to use any other appropriate Rule in this document provided that it is stated which Rules have been applied to which item	D1 Fixtures, furnishings, equipment, fittings and appliances consist of those items listed as Sections N10 – 13, N15, N20 – 23 and Q50 at Appendix A excluding signwriting and carving and sculpting		S1 Such information as is appropriate to the procurement, design, execution, supply and/or manufacture of the item and its incorporation in the Works
	2 Dimensioned diagram						S2 Details of excavation and concrete backfilling for foundations to Site/Street furniture/equipment
2 Signwriting	1 Dimensioned description						S3 Specified codes of practice and regulations
3 Carving and sculpting							S4 Kind and quality of materials
4 Fittings, equipment and appliances associated with services	1 Type, size and pattern, capacity, loading as appropriate and method of fixing all stated	1 Cross reference to specification	nr	M2 Marking positions, loose ancillaries, identification, testing and commissioning, temporary operation, preparing drawings, operating and maintenance manuals are measured in Sections Y51, Y54 and Y59 as appropriate		C1 Providing everything necessary for jointing is deemed to be included	S5 Gauge, thickness or substance of materials
		1 Ancillaries provided with fittings, equipment and appliances, details stated					S6 Tests with which materials and equipment must comply
		2 Integral controls and indicators stated					
		3 Remote controls and indicators and connections between, details stated					

				4 Supports, mountings and insulation provided with fittings, equipment and appliances, details stated	S7 Finishes or surface treatments applied on site
				5 Initial charges, details stated	S8 Finishes and surface treatments applied off site stating whether applied before or after fabricating or assembly
				6 Method of fixing and background stated	S9 Limiting dimensions on the size and weight of equipment
5 Ancillaries not provided with the fittings, equipment or appliances	1 Type, size and method of jointing stated	1 Type of fitting, equipment or appliance stated	nr	1 Integral controls or indicators stated	C2 Jointing ancillaries to fittings, equipment or appliances is deemed to be included
				2 Remote controls or indicators and connections between, details stated	
6 Fixtures, furnishings, equipment, fittings and appliances provided by the Employer	1 Type, size and method of fixing stated		nr	1 Provision of additional components, details stated	C3 Accepting delivery, storing and handling are deemed to be included
				2 Background stated	

P Building fabric sundries

P10 Sundry insulation/proofing work/fire stops

	MEASUREMENT RULES	DEFINITION RULES	COVERAGE RULES	SUPPLEMENTARY INFORMATION
INFORMATION PROVIDED P1 Information is shown on location drawings under A Preliminaries/General conditions		D1 Sundry insulation/proofing work/fire stops include: (a) flexible sheets, insulating boards and other materials, where not specified as part of another section, laid, hung or fixed horizontally, sloping or vertically as waterproofing, vapour barriers, fire stops, fire barriers, isolating membranes, sound insulation or thermal insulation (b) mineral fibre, plastics bead and cellulose loose fill thermal insulation laid between joists, etc.		

CLASSIFICATION TABLE

				MEASUREMENT RULES	DEFINITION RULES	COVERAGE RULES	SUPPLEMENTARY INFORMATION
1 Sheets 2 Quilts 3 Boards 4 Loose fill	1 Plain areas 2 Across members, centres of members stated 3 Between members, centres of members stated	1 Horizontal 2 Vertical 3 Soffit	m²	M1 The area measured is that covered M2 Proofing work/fire stops are only measured independently in this Section where not specified as part of another Work Section	D2 Horizontal includes the upper surface of any sloping structure ≤ 45° from the horizontal D3 Vertical includes the upper surface of any sloping structure > 45° from the horizontal D4 Soffit includes the underside of any horizontal or sloping structure	C1 All cutting is deemed to be included	S1 Type, quality and thickness of material S2 Extent of laps S3 Method of fixing where not at the discretion of the Contractor

P11 Foamed/Fibre/Bead cavity wall insulation

	INFORMATION PROVIDED
P1	Information is shown on location drawings under A Preliminaries/General conditions

			MEASUREMENT RULES	DEFINITION RULES	COVERAGE RULES	SUPPLEMENTARY INFORMATION
CLASSIFICATION TABLE				D1 Foamed/Fibre/Bead cavity wall insulation includes foamed resin or loose fill insulation injected or blown into cavity walls		S1 Type and quality of material
1 Filling	1 Thickness stated	m²	M1 The area measured is that filled			S2 Method of application including associated works

	INFORMATION PROVIDED
	P1 Information is shown on location drawings under A Preliminaries/General conditions

CLASSIFICATION TABLE

Classification			Measurement unit		MEASUREMENT RULES	DEFINITION RULES	COVERAGE RULES	SUPPLEMENTARY INFORMATION
1 Skirtings, picture rails, architraves and the like	1 Dimensioned overall cross-section description		m	1 Built up timber members, size of components stated	M1 Items which do not have a constant cross-section are so described and given stating the extreme dimensions	D1 All timber sizes are nominal sizes unless stated as finished sizes	C1 The work is deemed to include ends, angles, mitres, intersections and the like except on hardwood items > 0.003 m² sectional area	S1 Kind and quality of materials and if timber whether sawn or wrot
2 Cover fillets, stops, trims, beads, nosings and the like				2 Timber components tongued on	M2 Items are only measured independently in this Section where not specified as part of another Work Section			S2 Preservative treatments applied as part of the production process
3 Isolated shelves and worktops				3 Different cross-section shapes (nr)	M3 Curved work is so described with the radii stated			S3 Surface treatments applied as part of the production process
4 Window boards				4 Stopped labours (nr)	M4 Associated handrails are measured in Section L30 and Section L31			S4 Selection and protection for subsequent treatment
5 Unframed pinboards			nr					S5 Matching grain or colour
6 Duct covers								S6 Limits on planing margins on timber and if deviation from stated size is not permitted
7 Isolated handrails and grab rails		1 Ends	nr	1 Built up timber members, size of components stated				S7 Method of joining or form of construction
		2 Angles		2 Timber components tongued on				S8 Method of fixing where not at the discretion of the Contractor
8 Extra over the hardwood items, > 0.003 m² sectional area, in which they occur		3 Mitres		3 Stopped labours (nr)				S9 Fixing through vulnerable materials
9 Backboards, plinth blocks and the like	1 Dimensioned description	4 Intersections						

P21 Ironmongery

INFORMATION PROVIDED			MEASUREMENT RULES	DEFINITION RULES	COVERAGE RULES	SUPPLEMENTARY INFORMATION
P1 Information is shown on location drawings under A Preliminaries/General conditions						
CLASSIFICATION TABLE						
1 Type of item, unit or set stated	1 Nature of base stated	nr		D1 Ironmongery consists of the items listed as Section P21 at Appendix A of these rules	C1 Ironmongery is deemed to include fixing with screws to match and preparing base to receive same	S1 Kind and quality of materials and fixings S2 Surface finish S3 Constituent parts of the units or sets S4 Fixing through vulnerable materials

INFORMATION PROVIDED

P1 The following information is shown on location drawings under A Preliminaries/General conditions or on further drawings which accompany the bills of quantities
(a) scope and location of the work

CLASSIFICATION TABLE

Classification			Unit		MEASUREMENT RULES	DEFINITION RULES	COVERAGE RULES	SUPPLEMENTARY INFORMATION
1 Joints, contact surfaces stated	1 Type and size of components stated	1 Vertical 2 Sloping 3 Soffit 4 Horizontal	m	1 Raking out existing materials	M1 Lengths are measured on face	D1 Sealant joints include forming sealant joints which for special reasons cannot reasonably be included in another Work Section as follows: (a) general expansion joints in the building not associated with any particular type of work (b) sealant joints required to be executed by a sealant specialist (c) renewal of sealant joints in existing buildings where not associated with replacement or refixing of a component	C1 Work is deemed to include preparation, cleaners, primers and sealers appropriate to the contact surface C2 Raking out existing materials is deemed to include raking out/cutting back the existing components sufficiently to accommodate the new system, disposal, and any make up filler where excess is removed	S1 Kind and quality of materials S2 Method of application S3 Preparation of contact surfaces, cleaners, primers and sealers
2 Pointing, contact surfaces stated			m			D2 Vertical joints include work inclined ≤ 10° from vertical D3 Sloping joints include work to upper surfaces inclined > 10° from horizontal and > 10° from vertical D4 Soffit joints include all inclined soffits D5 Horizontal joints include work inclined ≤ 10° from horizontal		

INFORMATION PROVIDED

P1 Information regarding the nature of excavation work is described in accordance with Section D20, Information Provided

P2 The following information is shown either on location drawings under A Preliminaries/General conditions or on further drawings which accompany the bills of quantities:

(a) the layout of the services

CLASSIFICATION TABLE

1 Excavating trenches	1 Services ≤ 200 mm nominal size	1 Average depth of run ≤ 250 mm	m	1 Commencing level stated where > 0.25 m below existing ground level	D1 Trenches next to roadways, next to existing buildings, and in unstable ground are defined in accordance with D20:7.*.*.3 – 5	C1 Excavating trenches are deemed to include: (a) earthwork support (b) consolidation of trench bottoms (c) trimming excavations (d) special protection of services (e) backfilling with and compaction of excavated materials (f) disposal of surplus excavated materials	S2 Specified protection where required
	2 Services > 200 mm nominal size, nominal size stated	2 and thereafter in 250 mm stages		2 Curved	D2 Backfilling with special materials occurs where selected or treated excavated materials, or imported materials are used		
				3 Below ground water level			
				4 Next to roadways			
				5 Next to existing buildings			
				6 Unstable ground			
				7 Specified multiple handling details stated			
				8 Disposal at specified locations, details stated			
				9 Backfilling with special materials, details stated			
				10 Surface treatment, details stated			

MEASUREMENT RULES

M1 Unless identified in these sections all other items of Builder's work associated with plumbing, mechanical and electrical installations are given in accordance with the appropriate Work Sections

M2 Builder's work in connection with plumbing, mechanical and electrical installations are each identified under an appropriate heading

M3 Special materials for backfilling are stated in accordance with Section D20:9.*.*.*

M4 Surface treatments are stated in accordance with D20:13.*.*.*

M5 Excavating trenches below ground water level is measured where the ground water level is above the bottom of the trench

DEFINITION RULES (see table above, D1, D2)

COVERAGE RULES (see table above, C1)

SUPPLEMENTARY INFORMATION

S1 Kind and quality of materials

S2 Specified protection where required

CLASSIFICATION TABLE					MEASUREMENT RULES	DEFINITION RULES	COVERAGE RULES	SUPPLEMENTARY INFORMATION
2 Items extra over excavating trenches, irrespective of depth	1 Breaking out existing materials	1 Rock 2 Concrete 3 Reinforced concrete 4 Brickwork, blockwork or stonework 5 Coated macadam or asphalt		m³	M6 The measurement of extra over items is based on the width of the beds in the trenches. Where there are no beds the width to be taken is the nominal size of the service plus 300 mm. In both cases measurement is subject to a minimum width of 500 mm	D3 Rock is any material which is of such a size or position that it can only be removed by wedges, special plant or explosives		
	2 Breaking out existing hard pavings, thickness stated			m²				
	3 Lifting turf for preservation	1 Method of preserving, details stated	1 Reinstating to match existing	m²				
	4 Next existing live services	1 Type and number of services stated		nr				
	5 Around existing live services crossing trench			item	M7 To be measured where precautions are specifically required			S3 Nature of special requirement
3 Disposal	1 Surface water 2 Ground water			item	M8 An item for disposal of ground water is only measured where a corresponding item is measured in accordance with 1.✳.3 and is adjusted accordingly if the post contract water level is different	D4 Surface water is water on the surface of the site and the excavations		
4 Beds	1 Width and thickness of bed stated			m			C2 Beds, haunchings, surrounds and casings are deemed to include formwork	
5 Beds and haunchings	1 Width and thickness of bed stated			m				
6 Beds and surrounds	1 Width, thickness of bed and thickness of surround stated			m				
7 Vertical casings	1 Nominal size of service stated			m				
8 Stop cock pits, valve chambers and the like	1 Size stated			nr				
9 Other chambers	1 Type, size and method of construction stated			nr	M9 Other chambers are measured in accordance with the Section R12 rules for manholes			

Item	First division	Second division	Unit	Third division	Rules
10 Underground ducts for engineering services	1 Straight 2 Curved, radii stated 3 Flexible	1 Type, nominal size and method of jointing stated	m	1 Handed to others for laying	D5 Ducts include trays, trunking, gratings and the like
11 Items extra over the duct in which they occur	1 Fittings 2 Special treatment at ends	1 Description and method of jointing stated	nr		
12 Cover tiles 13 Identification tapes	1 Straight 2 Curved, radii stated	1 Type and size stated	m	1 Use of special colours for differing services 2 Staged laying 3 Handed to others for laying	
14 Marker posts 15 Marker plates	1 Type and size stated		nr	1 Lettering required	
16 Surface boxes 17 Access chambers 18 Inspection chambers	1 Type, size and covers stated	1 Bedding, and jointing, details stated 2 Handed to others for fixing	nr	1 Setting in hole, concrete or other material 2 Fixing to walls or other surfaces 3 Handed to others for setting or fixing	
19 Cutting or forming holes, mortices, sinkings and chases for electrical installations	1 Concealed conduits, type stated 2 Concealed cables, type stated 3 Exposed conduits, type stated 4 Exposed cables, type stated	1 Luminaire points 2 Socket outlet points 3 Fitting outlet points 4 Equipment and control gear points 5 Any point in unusually expensive coverings	nr	1 Making good 2 Making good vulnerable materials, details stated	M10 Points are enumerated irrespective of size, type and kind C3 Associated switch points are deemed to be included
20 Cutting or forming holes for other services installations	1 Ducts, nature and thickness of structure stated 2 Pipes, nature and thickness of structure stated	1 Girth ≤ 1.00 m 2 Girth 1.00 – 2.00 m 3 and thereafter in 1.00 m stages 1 ≤ 55 mm nominal size 2 55-110 mm nominal size 3 > 110 mm nominal size	nr	1 Rectangular 2 Circular 3 Dimensioned profile and description 4 Making good	D6 Pipes include tubes, bars, cables, conduit and the like

	CLASSIFICATION TABLE				MEASUREMENT RULES	DEFINITION RULES	COVERAGE RULES	SUPPLEMENTARY INFORMATION
21 Cutting or forming mortices, sinkings and the like for other services installations	1 Size stated	1 Nature of structure stated		nr			1 Making good	
22 Cutting or forming chases for other services installations	1 Number and size of services stated			m				
23 Pipe and duct sleeves	1 Building in	1 Type, size of pipe or duct and nature of structure stated		nr			1 Fix only 2 Bedding and pointing 3 Fire resistant packing 4 Water proofing 5 Making good 6 Method of fixing stated	
	2 Other fixing			m				
24 Ends of supports for services equipment, fittings, appliances and ancillaries	1 Type and size of support stated			nr				
25 Ends of supports for pipes and ducts	1 Pipes and ducts ≤ 55 mm nominal size	1 Grouped together stating spacing of supports		m	M11 Measured net length of pipe or duct over all fittings		1 Fix only 2 Bedding and pointing 3 Making good 4 Method of fixing and background stated	
	2 Pipes and ducts > 55 mm nominal size	2 Size and type of pipe or duct stated		nr				
26 Special measures where services pass through walls, floors, ceilings and roofs	1 Type of measure and size stated	1 Method of fixing and nature of structure stated		nr		D7 Special measures include precautions against the spread of fire and water		
27 Trench covers and frames	1 Type and width stated	1 Method of fixing and background stated		m			1 Limitations to length of covers stated	
28 Duct covers and frames	1 Type and size stated	1 Method of fixing and background stated		m				
29 Blockings, grounds and fixings for services	1 Type and size stated	1 Method of fixing and nature of structure stated		nr				

					Rules
30 Supports for services not provided with the services installation	1 Pylons 2 Poles 3 Wall and soffit brackets and hangers 4 Pole brackets 5 Stays 6 Proprietary support components	1 Type, size and method of fixing and background stated	nr	1 Holes, pits and bedding	
31 Catenary cables	1 Type and size stated	1 Method of fixing and background stated	m	1 Eye bolts, details stated 2 Shackles, details stated 3 Straining screws, details stated	M12 Measured net, no allowance for sag
Work to existing buildings					
32 Cutting mortices and sinkings for services installations	1 Size stated	1 Nature of structure stated	nr	1 Making good, details stated	M13 Cutting holes for services installations and making good after is measured in accordance with the appropriate Work Sections
33 Cutting chases for services installations	1 Number and size of services installations		m		
34 Lifting and replacing floor boards	1 For pipes or ducts 2 For cables or conduits	1 Number and nominal size of pipe or duct stated 2 ≤ 3 cables or conduits 3 3 – 6 cables or conduits 4 > 6 cables or conduits	m		M14 No distinction is made between routes parallel to or at an angle to the floor boards C4 Cutting floor boards and notching or holing joists are deemed to be included
35 Lifting and replacing chequer plates, trench covers and duct covers	1 Type and width stated		m		

Q10 Stone/Concrete/Brick kerbs/edgings/channels

INFORMATION PROVIDED

P1 The following information is shown either on location drawings under A Preliminaries/General conditions or on further drawings which accompany the bills of quantities:

(a) the scope and location of the work

CLASSIFICATION TABLE

			MEASUREMENT RULES	DEFINITION RULES	COVERAGE RULES	SUPPLEMENTARY INFORMATION
			M1 In situ concrete kerbs/edgings/channels to in situ concrete roads are measured in Section Q21			
1 Excavation			M2 Excavation work is measured in accordance with Section D20			
2 Kerbs 3 Edgings 4 Channels	1 Dimensioned description	m	1 Sizes and extent of reinforcement 2 Foundation and haunching 3 Curved, radii stated	M3 Where otherwise identical units are required which vary in their length, the number of units is to be stated in the item	C1 Kerbs, edgings and channels are deemed to include cut angles and ends C2 Foundation and haunching is deemed to include formwork	S1 Kind and quality of materials S2 Mix details S3 Bedding and fixings S4 Surface finishes S5 Nature and extent of foundation and haunching
5 Items extra over the work in which they occur	1 Specials	nr				

Q21 In situ concrete roads/pavings/bases

P1 The following information is shown either on location drawings under A Preliminaries/General conditions or on further drawings
   which accompany the bills of quantities:
   (a) the scope and location of the work

CLASSIFICATION TABLE

			MEASUREMENT RULES	DEFINITION RULES	COVERAGE RULES	SUPPLEMENTARY INFORMATION
1 Concrete			M1 Concrete is measured in accordance with Section E10			
2 Formwork			M2 Formwork is measured in accordance with Section E20			
3 Reinforcement			M3 Reinforcement is measured in accordance with Section E30			
4 Joints			M4 Joints are measured in accordance with Section E40			
5 Worked finishes			M5 Worked finishes are measured in accordance with Section E41			
6 Accessories cast in			M6 Accessories cast in are measured in accordance with Section E42			

Q22 Coated macadam/Asphalt roads/pavings

INFORMATION PROVIDED

P1 The following information is shown either on location drawings under A Preliminaries/General conditions or on further drawings which accompany the bills of quantities:

(a) the scope and location of the work

CLASSIFICATION TABLE

				MEASUREMENT RULES	DEFINITION RULES	COVERAGE RULES	SUPPLEMENTARY INFORMATION
1 Roads	1 Thickness and number of coats stated	1 Level and to falls only	m²	M1 The area measured is that in contact with the base and no deduction is made for voids ≤ 0.50 m² or grounds	D1 Work is deemed external unless described as internal	C1 Work is deemed to include: (a) fair joints (b) working over and around obstructions into recesses and shaped inserts	S1 Kind, composition and mix of materials S2 Method of application S3 Nature of surface treatment S4 Special curing of finished work S5 Nature of base S6 Preparatory work where bonding is included with the finish
2 Pavings		2 To falls and crossfalls and to slopes ≤ 15° from horizontal	m²		D2 The thickness stated is the finished thickness	C2 Work is deemed to include forming or working into shallow channels and associated labours	
		3 To slopes > 15° from the horizontal	m²			C3 Work to falls and crossfalls, and to slopes is deemed to include intersections	
3 Linings to channels	1 Horizontal	1 Girth on face stated	m			C4 Linings to channels are deemed to include arrises, coves, ends, angles, intersections and outlets	
	2 To falls						

Q23 Gravel/Hoggin roads/pavings

INFORMATION PROVIDED

P1 The following information is shown either on location drawings under A Preliminaries/General conditions or on further drawings which accompany the bills of quantities:

(a) the scope and location of the work

CLASSIFICATION TABLE

					MEASUREMENT RULES	DEFINITION RULES	COVERAGE RULES	SUPPLEMENTARY INFORMATION
1 Roads 2 Pavings	1 Thickness stated	1 Level and to falls only 2 To falls and crossfalls and to slopes ≤ 15° from horizontal 3 To slopes > 15° from horizontal	m^2		M1 Area measured is that in contact with base and no deduction is made for voids ≤ 0.50 m^2	D1 Work is deemed external unless described as internal D2 The thickness stated is the compacted thickness	C1 The work is deemed to include: (a) fair joints (b) working over and around obstructions into recesses and shaped inserts	S1 Kind and quality of materials S2 Formation, preparation and surface finish or treatment S3 Laying and compaction
3 Edgings	1 Thickness and height stated		m				C2 Edgings are deemed to include: (a) pegs and supports (b) angles and ends	S4 Type and method of fixing or support

Q24 Interlocking brick/block roads/pavings
Q25 Slab/Brick/Block/Sett/Cobble pavings

INFORMATION PROVIDED

P1 The following information is shown either on location drawings under A Preliminaries/General conditions or on further drawings which accompany the bills of quantities:
(a) the scope and location of the work

CLASSIFICATION TABLE

Classification			Unit	MEASUREMENT RULES	DEFINITION RULES	COVERAGE RULES	SUPPLEMENTARY INFORMATION
1 Roads	1 Thickness stated	1 Level and to falls only	m²	M1 Work is measured on the exposed face and no deduction is made for voids ≤ 0.50 m²	D1 Work is deemed external unless otherwise described	C1 Work is deemed to include: (a) fair joints (b) working over and around obstructions into recesses and shaped inserts (c) cutting	S1 Kind and quality of materials including bedding
2 Pavings		2 To falls and crossfalls and to slopes ≤ 15° from the horizontal			D2 The thickness stated is the nominal thickness	C2 Work is deemed to include forming or working finishes into shallow channels including all associated labours	S2 Size, shape and thickness of units
		3 To slopes > 15° from the horizontal				C3 Work to falls and crossfalls and to slopes ≤ 15° is deemed to include all intersections	S3 Nature of surface finish
		1 Bedding, thickness stated					S4 Bedding or other method of fixing
		2 Patterned, details stated					S5 Treatment of joints
		3 Work with joints laid out to detail, components detail drawing reference stated					S6 Layout of joints
		4 Laid in bays, average size of bays stated					S7 Nature of base
							S8 Preparatory work
3 Treads	1 Width stated	1 Patterned, details stated	m			C4 Work is deemed to include all fair edges, internal and external angles	
4 Margins		2 Foundation and haunching					
		3 Curved, radii stated					
5 Risers	1 Height stated		m				
6 Kerbs	1 Dimensioned description		m	M2 Kerbs, edgings and channels in a similar material to the roads/pavings are measured here. Independent kerbs, edgings and channels are measured in Section Q10		C5 Linings to channels are deemed to include edges, angles, intersections and outlets	S9 Nature and extent of foundation and haunching
7 Edgings						C6 Foundation and haunching is deemed to include formwork	
8 Linings to channels	1 Girth on face stated						
9 Items extra over the work in which they occur	1 Special units	1 Dimensioned description	m				
	2 Isolated special units	1 Curved, radii stated	nr				
10 Accessories	1 Separating membranes	1 Thickness stated	m²		D4 Movement joints include expansion joints		
	2 Movement joints	1 Dimensioned description	m				
	3 Tree grilles		nr				

Q26 Special surfacings/pavings for sport

INFORMATION PROVIDED

P1 The following information is shown either on location drawings under A Preliminaries/General conditions or on further drawings which accompany the bills of quantities:
(a) the scope and location of the work

CLASSIFICATION TABLE

Classification	Sub-classification	Unit
1 Liquid applied surfacings	1 Level and to falls only	m²
	2 To falls and crossfalls and to slopes ≤ 15° from the horizontal	
	3 To slopes > 15° from the horizontal	
2 Sheet surfacings	1 Thickness stated	m²
3 Tufted surfacings		
4 Proprietary coloured tarmacadam sports surfacings and pavings	1 Thickness and number of coats stated	m²
5 Proprietary clay and shale coloured sports surfacings and pavings		
6 Proprietary no fines concrete sports surfacings and pavings	1 Thickness stated	m²
7 Surface dressings		
8 Line marking	1 Width ≤ 300 mm	m
	2 Width > 300 mm, width stated	
9 Letters and figures	1 Dimensioned description	nr

MEASUREMENT RULES

M1 The area measured is that in contact with the base and no deduction is made for voids ≤ 0.50 m²

DEFINITION RULES

D1 Work is deemed external unless described as internal

D2 The thickness stated is the nominal thickness

COVERAGE RULES

C1 Work is deemed to include:
(a) fair joints
(b) working over and around obstructions into recesses and shaped inserts
(c) cutting

C2 Work is deemed to include forming or working into shallow channels and associated labours

C3 Work to falls and crossfalls and slopes is deemed to include intersections

SUPPLEMENTARY INFORMATION

S1 Kind and quality of materials
S2 Nature of base
S3 Number of coats
S4 Surface finish
S5 Method of application
S6 Methods of fixing and treatment of joints
S7 Extent of laps
S8 Type of seams
S9 Proprietary name
S10 Method of application
S11 Surface treatment
S12 Preparatory work
S13 Coats (nr)
S14 Method of application
S15 Treatment applied between coats

Q30 Seeding/Turfing

INFORMATION PROVIDED

P1 The following information is shown either on location drawings under A Preliminaries/General conditions or on further drawings which accompany the bills of quantities:
(a) the scope and location of the work

CLASSIFICATION TABLE

			MEASUREMENT RULES	DEFINITION RULES	COVERAGE RULES	SUPPLEMENTARY INFORMATION
1 Cultivating	1 Depth stated					
2 Surface applications	1 Type and rate stated					
3 Seeding	1 Rate stated					
4 Turfing						
5 Turfing edges of seeded areas	1 Width stated	m²				
6 Protection	1 Temporary fencing					
	1 Weeding, details stated					
	2 Cutting, details stated					
	3 Preparatory work, details stated					
	1 Duration and ultimate ownership, details stated		M1 Protective temporary fencing is only measured here where specifically required and then in accordance with Section Q40	D1 Types of surface applications include herbicides, selective weedkillers, peat, manure, compost, mulch, fertilizer, soil ameliorants, sand and the like	C1 Cultivating is deemed to include the removal of stones C2 Surface applications are deemed to include working in if required C3 Seeding is deemed to include raking or harrowing in and rolling C4 Cutting is deemed to include edge trimming	S1 Timing of operations S2 Method of cultivating and degree of tilth S3 Kind, quality, composition and mix of materials S4 Method of application S5 Method of securing turves

Q31 Planting

INFORMATION PROVIDED

P1 The following information is shown either on location drawings under A Preliminaries/General conditions or on further drawings which accompany the bills of quantities:
(a) the scope and location of the work

	MEASUREMENT RULES	DEFINITION RULES	COVERAGE RULES	SUPPLEMENTARY INFORMATION

CLASSIFICATION TABLE

First	Second	Third	Unit	Supplementary information
1 Cultivating	1 Depth stated		m²	1 Weeding, details stated
				2 Fallowing, details stated
2 Surface applications	1 Type and rate stated		m²	
3 Trees	1 Botanical name	1 BS size designation and root system stated	nr	1 Planting in cultivated or grassed areas prepared by others, details stated
		2 Girth, height and clear stem and root system stated	nr	2 Initial cut back, details stated
4 Young nursery stock trees		1 Height and root system stated	nr	3 Supports and ties
5 Shrubs		1 Height stated	nr	4 Refilling with special materials, details stated
		2 Height, spacing, number of rows, and layout stated	m	5 Watering, details stated
6 Hedge plants		1 Size stated	nr	
		2 Size and number per m² stated	m²	
7 Herbaceous plants		1 Size stated	nr	
8 Bulbs, corms and tubers		1 Size stated	nr / kg	
9 Mulching after planting	1 Around individual plants	1 Thickness and area stated	nr	1 Tree spats, details stated
	2 Beds	2 Thickness stated	m²	
10 Protection	1 Tree guards	1 Dimensioned description	nr	
	2 Anti-desiccant sprays	2 Height and girth of tree or spread of plant stated	nr	
	3 Wrapping	3 Height of wrapping and girth of tree stated	nr	
	4 Temporary fencing			1 Duration and ultimate ownership, details stated

M1 Temporary fencing is only measured here where specifically required and then in accordance with Section Q40

Deemed to be / Definition rules

C1 Cultivating is deemed to include the removal of stones

C2 Surface applications are deemed to include working in if required

C3 Items include for excavating or forming pits, holes or trenches, refilling, watering in, removing surplus excavated material

C4 Refilling is deemed to include all necessary multiple handling

C5 Planting in cultivated or grassed areas prepared by others is deemed to include all necessary reinstatement

D1 Types of surface applications include herbicides, selective weedkillers, peat, manure, compost, mulch, fertilizer, soil ameliorants, sand and the like

D2 BS size designations include standard, advanced nursery stock or semi-mature trees

D3 Young nursery stock includes seedlings, transplants and whips

D4 Removing surplus excavated material means removing from site unless otherwise described

Supplementary information

S1 Timing of operations

S2 Method of cultivating and degree of tilth

S3 Kind, quality and composition of materials

S4 Size and type of pits, holes and trenches, excavated or formed

S5 Type of supports and ties

S6 Special materials for refilling

S7 Labelling

S8 Type of mulch, time and method of application

S9 Type of tree guard and method of fixing

S10 Type of spray and rate of application

S11 Type of wrapping and chemical application

INFORMATION PROVIDED

P1 The following information is shown either on location drawings under A Preliminaries/General conditions or on further drawings which accompany the bills of quantities:

(a) the scope and location of the work

(b) location of fencing specially designed to suit sloping ground

CLASSIFICATION TABLE

			Unit	
1 Fencing	1 Type stated	1 Height of fencing; spacing, height and depth of supports stated	m	1 Fencing set out to a curve but straight between posts
				2 Curved fencing radius > 100 m
				3 Curved fencing radius ≤ 100 m, radii stated
				4 Fencing to ground sloping > 15° from the horizontal
				5 Lengths ≤ 3 m
2 Special supports extra over fencing in which they occur	1 End posts	1 Size, height and depth stated	nr	1 Method of fixing to background and background stated
	2 Angle posts			2 Details of struts or backstays stated
	3 Integral gate posts			
	4 Straining posts			
	5 Others, details stated			
3 Independent gate posts	1 Type stated			

MEASUREMENT RULES

M1 Fencing is measured over supports and special supports

DEFINITION RULES

D1 Supports are posts, struts or the like occurring at regular intervals

D2 Special supports are posts, struts or the like other than those occurring at regular intervals

D3 The height of fencing is measured from the surface of the ground (or other stated base) to the top of the infilling or where there is no infilling, to the top wire or rail

D4 Curved fencing is fencing curved between supports

D5 Integral gate posts are those integral with the fencing

D6 The height of supports and special supports is the height above the surface of the ground or other stated base

D7 The depth of supports and special supports is the depth below the surface of the ground or other stated base

COVERAGE RULES

C1 Work is deemed to include:

(a) excavating holes for supports, special supports and independent gate posts

(b) backfilling and disposal of surplus materials

(c) earthwork support

(d) supports

C2 Gate posts are deemed to include slamming stops and hanging fillets

SUPPLEMENTARY INFORMATION

S1 Kind and quality of materials

S2 Construction

S3 Surface treatments applied as part of production process or applied before delivery to site

S4 Size and nature of backfilling

			Unit			
4 Items extra over fencing, special supports and independent gate posts irrespective of type	1 Excavating below ground water level		m³	M2 If the post contract water level differs from the pre-contract water level the measurements are revised accordingly		C3 Disposal of ground water is deemed to be included
	2 Breaking out existing materials	1 Rock 2 Concrete 3 Reinforced concrete 4 Brickwork, blockwork or stonework 5 Coated macadam or asphalt	m²		D8 Rock is any material which is of such size or position that it can only be removed by wedges, special plant or explosives	C4 Making good existing hard pavings is deemed to be included
	3 Breaking out existing hard pavings, thickness stated					
5 Gates	1 Type stated	1 Height and width stated	nr			C5 Gates are deemed to include gate stops, gate catches and independent gate stays and their associated works
6 Ironmongery				M3 Ironmongery is measured in accordance with Section P21		

R Disposal systems

R10 Rainwater pipework/gutters
R11 Foul drainage above ground

INFORMATION PROVIDED		MEASUREMENT RULES	DEFINITION RULES	COVERAGE RULES	SUPPLEMENTARY INFORMATION
P1 The following information is shown either on location drawings under A Preliminaries/General conditions or on further drawings which accompany the bills of quantities: (a) the scope and location of the work			D1 Finishes and surface treatments exclude insulation and decorative finishes which are measured under Sections Y50 and M60	C1 Providing everything necessary for jointing is deemed to be included C2 Patterns, moulds, templates and the like are deemed to be included	S1 Specified codes of practice and regulations S2 Kind and quality of materials S3 Gauge, thickness or substance of materials S4 Tests with which materials must comply S5 Finishes or surface treatments applied on site S6 Finishes or surface treatments applied off site stating whether applied before or after fabrication or assembly

CLASSIFICATION TABLE

				MEASUREMENT RULES	DEFINITION RULES	COVERAGE RULES
1 Pipes	1 Straight 2 Curved, radii stated 3 Flexible 4 Extendable	m	1 Type, nominal size, method of jointing, type, spacing and method of fixing supports, all stated	1 Background and method of fixing stated 2 In ducts 3 In chases 4 In floor screeds 5 In in situ concrete	M1 Pipes are measured over all fittings and branches M2 Flexible pipes and extendable pipes are measured fully extended		C3 Pipes are deemed to include joints in their running length C4 Pipes are deemed to include joints necessary solely for erection purposes C5 Pipes are deemed to include all labour excluding made bends
2 Items extra over the pipe in which they occur	1 Made bends 2 Special joints and connections	nr	1 Type, and method of jointing stated	1 Nominal size stated where different from pipe in which joint or connection occurs		D2 Special joints and connections are joints which differ from those generally occurring in the running length or are connections to pipes of a different profile or material, connections to existing pipes or to equipment, appliances or ends of flue pipes	

First column	Second column	Third column	Unit	Supplementary information	Measurement rules	Coverage rules
	3 Fittings, pipe ≤ 65 mm diameter	1 One end 2 Two ends 3 Three ends 4 Others, details stated	nr	1 With inspection door 2 Method of jointing stated where different from pipe in which fitting occurs	M3 Fittings which are reducing are measured extra over the largest pipe in which they occur	C6 Cutting and jointing pipes to fittings is deemed to be included
	4 Fittings, pipe > 65 mm diameter	5 Type stated	nr			
3 Screwed sockets 4 Tappings 5 Bosses	1 Type, size and method of jointing stated	1 Nominal size and kind of pipe stated	nr			C7 Screwed sockets, tappings and bosses are deemed to include perforating the pipe
6 Pipework ancillaries	1 Gullies 2 Outlets 3 Rainwater heads 4 Gratings to outlets and rainwater heads 5 Flashing plates 6 Weathering aprons 7 Tundishes 8 Traps 9 Pots	1 Type, nominal size, type of pipe, number and method of fixing any supports stated	nr	1 Background and method of fixing stated 2 In ducts	M4 Gratings may alternatively be given in the description of the enumerated item to which they relate	C8 Cutting and jointing pipes to ancillaries is deemed to be included
7 Pipe supports which differ from those given with pipelines		1 Nominal size of pipe, type and size of support, method of fixing pipe and support stated	nr	1 Lined with insulation, details stated 2 Background and method of fixing stated	M5 Fabricated supports and supports carrying more than one service are measured under Section P30/31	
8 Pipe sleeves through walls, floors and ceilings	1 Length ≤ 300 mm 2 and thereafter in 300 mm stages	1 Type and nominal size of pipe stated	nr	1 Method of fixing and type of packing stated 2 Handed to others for fixing		
9 Wall, floor and ceiling plates		1 Type, size and method of fixing stated	nr	1 Type, size and method of fixing stated		

CLASSIFICATION TABLE

No. / Feature	Classification 1	Classification 2	Unit	Classification 3	Supplementary	MEASUREMENT RULES	DEFINITION RULES	COVERAGE RULES	SUPPLEMENTARY INFORMATION
10 Gutters	1 Straight 2 Curved, radii stated	1 Type, nominal size, method of jointing, type, spacing and method of fixing supports stated	m	1 Background and method of fixing stated		M6 Gutters are measured over all fittings and branches		C9 Gutters are deemed to include joints in the running length	
11 Items extra over the gutter in which they occur	1 Special joints and connections	1 Type and method of jointing stated	nr	1 Nominal size stated where different from gutter in which joint or connection occurs			D3 Special joints and connections are joints which differ from those generally occurring in the running length or are connections to existing gutter or gutters of a different profile or material	C10 Cutting and jointing gutters to fittings is deemed to be included	
	2 Fittings	1 Type stated	nr	1 Method of jointing stated where different from gutter in which fitting occurs		M7 Fittings which are reducing are measured extra over the largest gutters in which they occur			
12 Marking position of holes, mortices and chases in the structure	1 Installation stated		item	1 Formed during construction, details stated					
13 Identification	1 Plates 2 Discs 3 Labels 4 Tapes or bands 5 Arrows, symbols, letters and numbers 6 Charts	1 Type, size and method of fixing stated	nr	1 Details of engraving stated 2 Mounting of charts, details stated					
14 Testing and commissioning	1 Installation stated		item	1 Preparatory operations, details stated 2 Stage tests (nr) listed and purpose stated 3 Insurance Company tests, details stated 4 Instruction of personnel in operation of completed installation	1 Attendance required 2 Instruments to be provided			C11 Provision of water, and other supplies are deemed to be included C12 Provision of test certificates is deemed to be included	
15 Temporary operation of installations to Employer's requirements	1 Installation and purpose of operation stated		item	1 Duration of operation period stated	1 Attendance required 2 Conditions imposed by Employer before operation allowed 3 Special insurance requirements of Employer stated	M8 Provision of water, fuel, gas, electricity and other supplies is covered by Provisional Sums in Section A54			

16 Preparing drawings	1 Information required and number of copies stated	1 Negatives, prints and microfilms, details stated	1 Binding into sets, details stated 2 Names of recipients stated	D4 Drawings include Builder's work, manufacturer's and installation drawings and record or 'as fitted' drawings
17 Operating and maintenance manuals				

INFORMATION PROVIDED

P1 Information regarding the nature of excavation work is described in accordance with Section D20 Information Provided

P2 The following information is shown either on location drawings under A Preliminaries/General conditions or on further drawings which accompany the bills of quantities:

(a) the layout of the drainage

CLASSIFICATION TABLE

				Unit	MEASUREMENT RULES	DEFINITION RULES	COVERAGE RULES	SUPPLEMENTARY INFORMATION
1 Excavating trenches	1 Pipes ≤ 200 mm nominal size	1 Average depth of trench ≤ 250 mm	1 Commencing level stated where > 0.25 m below existing ground level	m	M1 Special materials for backfilling are stated in accordance with D20:9.*.*.*	D1 A run of pipe trench is an uninterrupted line of excavating such as between manholes or between an accessory and a manhole or between accessories	C1 Excavating trenches is deemed to include:	S1 Kind and quality of materials
	2 Pipes > 200 mm nominal size, nominal size stated	2 and thereafter in 250 mm stages	2 Curved		M2 Surface treatments are stated in accordance with D20:13.*.*.*		(a) earthwork support	S2 Specified protection where specified
			3 Below ground water level		M3 Excavating trenches below ground water level is measured where the ground water level is above the bottom of the trench	D2 Trenches next to roadways, next to existing buildings, and in unstable ground are defined in accordance with D20:7.*.*.3–5	(b) consolidation of trench bottoms	
			4 Next to roadways				(c) trimming excavations	
			5 Next to existing buildings				(d) filling with and compaction of general filling materials	
			6 Unstable ground				(e) disposal of surplus excavated materials	
			7 Specified multiple handling, details stated					
			8 Disposal at specified locations, details stated					
			9 Backfilling with special materials, details stated			D3 Backfilling with special materials occurs where selected or treated excavated materials, or imported materials are used		
			10 Surface treatments, details stated					
2 Items extra over excavating trenches, irrespective of depth	1 Breaking out existing materials	1 Rock		m³	M4 The measurement of extra over items is based on the width of the beds in the trenches. Where there are no beds the width to be taken is the nominal size of the service plus 300 mm. In both cases measurement is subject to a minimum width of 500 mm	D4 Rock is any material which is of such size or position that it can only be removed by wedges, special plant or explosives		
		2 Concrete						
		3 Reinforced concrete						
		4 Brickwork, blockwork or stonework						
		5 Coated macadam or asphalt						
	2 Breaking out existing hard pavings, thickness stated		1 Reinstating to match existing	m²				
	3 Lifting turf for preservation, details stated	1 Method of preserving, details stated						

Classification	First subdivision	Second subdivision	Unit	Measurement rules	Definition / Coverage rules	Special rules
						S3 Nature of special requirement
4 Next existing live services	1 Type of service stated		nr	M5 To be measured where precautions are specifically required	D5 Retaining a service is a precaution which is specifically required	
5 Around existing live services crossing trench			item			
3 Disposal	1 Surface water		item	M6 An item for disposal of ground water is only measured where a corresponding item is measured in accordance with 1.*.3 and is adjusted accordingly if the post contract water level is different		
	2 Ground water					
		1 Designed joints, details stated	m			
4 Beds	1 Width and thickness of bed stated				C2 Beds, haunchings, surrounds and casings are deemed to include formwork	
5 Beds and haunchings	1 Width, thickness of bed and thickness of surround stated	1 Nominal size of pipe stated	m			
6 Beds and surrounds						
7 Vertical casings	1 Size stated		m			
8 Pipes	1 Nominal size stated	1 In trenches	m	1 Iron pipes in runs ≤ 3 m long (nr)	C3 Pipes are deemed to include pipe supports	S4 Method of jointing pipes
		2 In ducts in the ground or below a floor		2 Not laid in bottom of trench, average depth stated in accordance with 1.*.*.		
		3 Bracketed off walls		3 Vertical		
		4 Suspended from soffits		4 Height > 3.50 m above floor level		
				M7 Pipes are measured over all fittings and branches		
9 Items extra over the pipe in which they occur	1 Pipe fittings	1 Description stated	nr		C4 Pipe fittings are deemed to include cutting and jointing pipes to fittings and providing everything necessary for jointing	S5 Method of jointing fittings and accessories to pipes
10 Pipe accessories	1 Type stated	1 Dimensioned description	nr		D6 Accessories include gullies, traps, inspection shoes, fresh air inlets, non-return flaps and the like	
					D7 Dimensions stated for accessories include the nominal size of each inlet and outlet	
					C5 Accessories are deemed to include jointing pipes thereto and bedding in concrete	

CLASSIFICATION TABLE				MEASUREMENT RULES	DEFINITION RULES	COVERAGE RULES	SUPPLEMENTARY INFORMATION
11 Manholes 12 Inspection chambers 13 Soakaways 14 Cesspits 15 Septic tanks	1 Excavation 2 Concrete 3 Formwork 4 Reinforcement 5 Brickwork 6 Rendered coatings			M8 Excavation, concrete, formwork, brickwork, rendered coatings and other work are measured in accordance with the rules for the appropriate Work Sections			
	7 Building in ends of pipes 8 Channels 9 Benching 10 Step irons 11 Covers 12 Intercepting traps 13 Others	1 Dimensioned description	nr			C6 Building in ends of pipes is deemed to include cutting pipes	
			1 Building in ends of pipes, details stated 2 Channels, details stated 3 Benching, details stated 4 Step irons, details stated 5 Covers, details stated 6 Intercepting traps, details stated	M9 Items 11–15,7–13.1.0 are only measured separately in non preformed systems			
	14 Preformed systems	1 Dimensioned description	nr				
16 Connecting to Local Authority's sewer	1 Details stated		item	M10 Connecting to Local Authority's sewer is only measured here where it is executed by the Contractor. Work by Statutory Authorities is measured in Section A53			
17 Testing and commissioning	1 Installation stated	1 Preparatory operations, details stated 2 Stage tests (nr) listed and purpose stated 3 Insurance Company tests, details stated 4 Instruction of personnel in operation of completed installations	item 1 Attendance required 2 Instruments to be provided			C7 Provision of water and other supplies is deemed to be included C8 Provision of test certificates is deemed to be included	

18 Preparing drawings	1 Information required and number of copies stated	1 Negatives, prints and microfilms, details stated	1 Binding into sets, details stated	D7 Drawings include Builder's work, manufacturer's and installation drawings and record or 'as fitted' drawings
			2 Names of recipients stated	
19 Operating and maintenance manuals				

X Transport systems

INFORMATION PROVIDED

P1 The following information is shown either on location drawings under A Preliminaries/General conditions or on further drawings which accompany the bills of quantities:
(a) the scope and location of the work, including extent of work in motor, machinery or plant rooms

CLASSIFICATION TABLE

Item	1	2	Unit	
1 Lifts 2 Escalators 3 Moving pavements 4 Hoists 5 Cranes 6 Travelling cradles 7 Goods distribution/Mechanised warehousing 8 Mechanical document conveying 9 Pneumatic document conveying 10 Automatic document filing and retrieval	1 Component drawing reference 2 Type, size, pattern, capacity, loading, length, floors served as appropriate, all stated	1 Cross reference to specification	nr	
11 Marking position of holes, mortices and chases in the structure	1 Installation stated		item	1 Formed during construction, details stated
12 Identification where not provided with equipment	1 Plates 2 Discs 3 Labels 4 Tapes or bands 5 Arrows, symbols, letters and numbers 6 Charts	1 Type, size and method of fixing stated	nr	1 Details of engraving stated 2 Mounting of charts, details stated

MEASUREMENT RULES

M1 It is permissible in respect of any individual item to use any other appropriate Rule in this document provided that it is stated which Rules have been applied to the item

M2 Work is classified in accordance with the following Work Sections and given under an appropriate Work Section heading:

X10 Lifts
X11 Escalators
X12 Moving pavements
X20 Hoists
X21 Cranes
X22 Travelling cradles
X23 Goods distribution /Mechanised warehousing
X30 Mechanical document conveying
X31 Pneumatic document conveying
X32 Automatic document filing and retrieval

DEFINITION RULES

COVERAGE RULES

SUPPLEMENTARY INFORMATION

S1 Such information as is appropriate to the procurement, design, execution, supply and/or manufacture of the item and its incorporation in the works

13 Testing and commissioning	1 Installation stated	1 Preparatory operations, details stated 2 Stage tests (nr) listed and purpose stated 3 Insurance Company tests, details stated 4 Instruction of personnel in operation of completed installation	item 1 Attendance required 2 Instruments to be provided		C1 Provision of electricity and other supplies is deemed to be included C2 Provision of test certificates is deemed to be included
14 Temporary operation of installations to Employer's requirements	1 Installation and purpose of operation stated	1 Duration of operation period stated	item 1 Attendance required 2 Conditions imposed by Employer before operation allowed 3 Special insurance requirements of Employer stated	M3 Provision of electricity and other supplies is covered by Provisional Sums in Section A54	
15 Preparing drawings	1 Information required and number of copies stated	1 Negatives, prints and microfilms, details stated	item 1 Binding into sets, details stated 2 Names of recipients stated		D1 Drawings include builder's work, manufacturer's and installation drawings and record or 'as fitted' drawings
16 Operating and maintenance manuals					

Y Mechanical and electrical services measurement

Y10 Pipelines
Y11 Pipeline ancillaries

INFORMATION PROVIDED

P1 The following information is shown either on location drawings under A Preliminaries/General conditions or on further drawings which accompany the bills of quantities:

(a) scope and location of the work including extent of work in plant rooms

CLASSIFICATION TABLE

1 Pipes			MEASUREMENT RULES	DEFINITION RULES	COVERAGE RULES	SUPPLEMENTARY INFORMATION
1 Straight	1 Type, nominal size, method of jointing, type, spacing and method of fixing supports stated	m	M1 Work related to these Sections is classified in accordance with Sections R14 and R20–U70 as Appendix B and given under an appropriate Work Section heading	D1 Finishes and surface treatments exclude insulation and decorative finishes which are measured under Sections Y50 and M60	C1 Providing everything necessary for jointing is deemed to be included	S1 Specified codes of practice and regulations
2 Curved, radii stated		1 Background stated	M2 Work in plant rooms is identified separately		C2 Patterns, moulds, templates and the like are deemed to be included	S2 Kind and quality of materials
3 Flexible		2 In ducts				S3 Gauge, thickness or substance of materials
4 Extendable		3 In trenches			C3 Pipes are deemed to include joints in their running length	S4 Tests with which materials must comply
5 Flow and return header pipes	2 Type, length and nominal size of main pipe, number, type, length and diameter of each branch pipe, method of construction and method of jointing ends, type, number and method of fixing supports stated	nr	M3 Pipes are measured over all fittings and branches		C4 Pipes are deemed to include joints necessary solely for erection purposes	S5 Finishes or surface treatments applied on site
		4 In chases	M4 Flexible and extendable pipes are measured fully extended			S6 Finishes or surface treatments applied off site stating whether applied before or after fabrication or assembly
		5 In floor screeds				
		6 In in situ concrete				

2 Items extra over the pipes in which they occur

First division	Second division	Third division	Supplementary information	Unit
1 Made bends				nr
2 Special joints and connections	1 Type and method of jointing stated	1 Nominal size stated where different from pipe in which joint or connection occurs		nr
3 Fittings, pipe ≤ 65 mm diameter,	2 One end 3 Two ends 4 Three ends 5 Others, details stated	1 With inspection door 2 Method of jointing stated where different from pipe in which fitting occurs		nr
4 Fittings, pipe > 65 mm diameter	6 Type stated			nr
3 Expansion loops	1 Limiting dimensions and expansion accommodated stated	1 Type, nominal size, method of jointing, type, number and method of fixing supports stated		nr
4 Expansion compensators	1 Expansion accommodated stated	1 Type, size and method of jointing stated		nr
5 Screwed sockets	1 Nominal size and kind of pipe stated		1 Background stated 2 In ducts 3 In trenches	nr
6 Tappings				
7 Bosses				
8 Pipework ancillaries	1 Type of pipe stated	1 Type, nominal size, method of jointing, type, number and method of fixing supports all stated	1 Integral controls or indicators stated 2 Remote controls or indicators and connections between stated 3 Background stated 4 In ducts 5 In trenches	nr

D2 Special joints and connections are joints which differ from those generally occurring in the running length or are connections to pipes of a different profile or material, connections to existing pipes or to equipment, appliances or ends of flue pipes

M5 Fittings which are reducing are measured extra over the largest pipe in which they occur

C5 Cutting and jointing pipes to fittings, loops and compensators is deemed to be included

C6 Screwed sockets, tappings and bosses are deemed to include perforating the pipe

C7 Cutting and jointing pipes to ancillaries is deemed to be included

CLASSIFICATION TABLE

CLASSIFICATION TABLE			MEASUREMENT RULES	DEFINITION RULES	COVERAGE RULES	SUPPLEMENTARY INFORMATION
9 Pipe supports which differ from those given with pipelines	1 Nominal size of pipe, type and size of support, method of fixing pipe and support stated	nr	1 Lined with insulation, details stated 2 Spring compensated, loading and movement accommodated stated	M6 Fabricated supports and supports carrying more than one service are measured in Section P31		
10 Pipe anchors and guides	1 Nominal size of pipe, type, size and composition, method of fixing pipe and anchors or guide stated	nr	3 Background stated			
11 Pipe sleeves through walls, floors and ceilings	1 Type and nominal size of pipe stated	nr	1 Method of fixing and type of packing stated 2 Handed to others for fixing			
	1 Length ≤ 300 mm 2 and thereafter in 300 mm stages					
12 Wall, floor and ceiling plates	1 Type, size and method of fixing stated	nr				

Y20 - Y25 General pipeline equipment
Y40 - Y46 General air ductline equipment
Y52 Vibration isolation mountings
Y53 Control components - mechanical

INFORMATION PROVIDED	CLASSIFICATION TABLE			MEASUREMENT RULES	DEFINITION RULES	COVERAGE RULES	SUPPLEMENTARY INFORMATION
P1 The following information is shown either on location drawings under A Preliminaries/General conditions or on further drawings which accompany the bills of quantities: (a) scope and location of the work including extent of work in plant rooms	1 Equipment	1 Type, size and pattern, rated duty, capacity, loading as appropriate and method of fixing all stated	1 Cross-reference to Specification	M1 Work related to these Sections is classified in accordance with Sections R14 – U70 as Appendix B and given under an appropriate Work Section heading M2 Work in plant rooms is identified separately	D1 Finishes and surface treatments exclude insulation and decorative finishes which are measured under Sections Y50 and M60	C1 Providing everything necessary for jointing is deemed to be included C2 Patterns, moulds, templates and the like are deemed to be included C3 Plates, discs and labels for identification provided with the equipment are deemed to be included	S1 Specified codes of practice and regulations S2 Kind and quality of materials S3 Gauge, thickness or substance of materials S4 Tests with which materials and equipment must comply S5 Finishes or surface treatments applied on site S6 Finishes or surface treatments applied off site stating whether applied before or after fabrication or assembly S7 Limiting dimensions on the size and weight of equipment
			nr				
		1 Ancillaries provided with equipment, details stated 2 Integral controls or indicators, details stated 3 Remote controls or indicators, and connections between, details stated 4 Supports, anti-vibration mountings, insulation provided with equipment, details and method of fixing stated 5 Initial charges, details stated 6 Background stated					

CLASSIFICATION TABLE					MEASUREMENT RULES	DEFINITION RULES	COVERAGE RULES	SUPPLEMENTARY INFORMATION
2 Ancillaries for equipment not provided with the equipment	1 Type, size and method of jointing stated	1 Type of equipment stated	nr	1 Integral controls or indicators, details stated 2 Remote controls or indicators, and connections between, details stated			C4 Jointing ancillaries to equipment is deemed to be included	
3 Sill heaters 4 Skirting heaters	1 Elements (nr)	1 Output, type, size and method of jointing stated	m					
	2 Casings	2 Type, size and method of jointing stated	m				C5 Edge sealing strips are deemed to be included	
5 Items extra over the sill or skirting heater casings in which they occur	1 Angle sections 2 Matching plates 3 Valve access covers 4 End covers	1 Type, size and method of jointing stated	nr					
6 Supports where not provided with the equipment	1 Type, size and method of fixing stated	1 Type, size and method of jointing stated	nr	1 Background stated				
7 Independent vertical steel chimneys	1 Height, internal diameter and method of jointing stated		nr	1 Base plates (nr) 2 Base plate templates (nr) 3 Linings (nr) 4 Claddings (nr) 5 Anchor bolts (nr) 6 Guy ropes (nr) 7 Ladders (nr) 8 Guard rails (nr) 9 Painters hooks (nr) 10 Cleaning doors (nr) 11 Cowls 12 Terminals	M3 Flue pipes are measured as pipelines in Section Y10			
8 Anti vibration mountings where not provided with the equipment	1 Type, size and method of fixing stated		nr	1 Background stated				
9 Anti vibration or sound insulation material	1 Plant bases		m²	1 Nature and thickness stated				
10 Disconnecting, setting aside and refixing for the conveniences of other trades	1 Type of equipment and purpose of disconnection stated		item	1 Handed to others for fixing				

INFORMATION PROVIDED

P1 The following information is shown either on location drawings under A Preliminaries/General conditions or on further drawings which accompany the bills of quantities:
(a) scope and location of the work, including extent of work in plant rooms

CLASSIFICATION TABLE

			Unit	
1 Ducting	1 Straight	1 Type, shape, size, method of jointing type, spacing and method of fixing supports stated	m	1 Background stated
	2 Curved, radii stated			
	3 Rectangular curved on wider side, radii stated			
	4 Rectangular curved on narrower side, radii stated			
	5 Flexible			
2 Items extra over the ducting in which they occur	1 Lining ducting internally	1 Type and thickness of lining material and internal size of ducting stated	m	
	2 Special joints and connections	1 Type, size, ducting size and method of jointing stated	nr	1 Size stated where different from duct in which joint or connection occurs
	3 Fittings	1 Type stated	nr	1 Method of jointing stated where different from duct in which fitting occurs
	4 Access openings and covers or doors	1 Type stated	nr	
	5 Nozzle outlets	1 Internal size of ducting stated	nr	
	6 Test holes and covers			
3 Turns and splitters where not provided with fittings	1 Type stated		nr	

MEASUREMENT RULES	DEFINITION RULES	COVERAGE RULES	SUPPLEMENTARY INFORMATION
M1 Work related to this Section is classified in accordance with Sections U10 – U70 as Appendix B and given under an appropriate Work Section heading	D1 Finishes and surface treatments exclude insulation and decorative finishes which are measured under Sections Y50 and M60	C1 Providing everything necessary for jointing is deemed to be included	S1 Specified codes of practice and regulations
M2 Work in plant rooms is identified separately		C2 Patterns, moulds templates and the like are deemed to be included	S2 Kind and quality of materials
M3 Ducting is measured over all fittings and branches			S3 Gauge, thickness or substance of materials
M4 Lining may alternatively be given in the description of the ducting		C3 Ducting is deemed to include: (a) joints in the running length (b) stiffeners	S4 Tests with which materials must comply
M5 Where there is a preponderance of fittings (e.g. in plant rooms) they may be enumerated separately as individual full cost items	D2 Special joints and connections are joints which differ from those generally occurring in the running length or are connections to ducting of a different profile or material or to equipment and appliances	C4 Access openings, nozzle outlets and test holes are deemed to include the stiffening of openings	S5 Finishes or surface treatments applied on site
		C5 Cutting and jointing ducts to fittings is deemed to be included	S6 Finishes or surface treatments applied off site stating whether applied before or after fabrication or assembly

Y30/Y31 continued

CLASSIFICATION TABLE

					MEASUREMENT RULES	DEFINITION RULES	COVERAGE RULES	SUPPLEMENTARY INFORMATION
4 Ancillaries	1 Type, size, method of jointing, type, number and method of fixing supports all stated	1 Type of ducting stated	nr	1 Integral controls and indicators, details stated 2 Remote controls and indicators and connections between, details stated 3 Background stated			C6 Cutting and jointing ducts to ancillaries is deemed to be included	
5 Breaking into existing ducts	1 Type, size and location of duct stated	1 Purpose of breaking in stated	item	1 Obtaining approval for isolation where necessary 2 Isolating existing duct 3 Preparing ends of existing for new work 4 Limitations to shut down period				
6 Ducting supports which differ from those given with ductline		1 Shape, size of duct, type and size of support, method of fixing duct and support stated	nr	1 Lined with insulation, details stated 2 Spring compensated, loading and movement accommodated stated 3 Background stated	M6 Fabricated supports and supports carrying more than one service are measured in Section P31			
7 Ducting sleeves through walls, floors and ceilings	1 ≤ 300 mm length 2 and thereafter in 300 mm stages	1 Type and size of ducting stated	nr	1 Method of fixing and type of packing stated 2 Handed to others for fixing				

Y50 Thermal insulation

INFORMATION PROVIDED

P1 The following information is shown either on location drawings under A Preliminaries/General conditions or on further drawings which accompany the bills of quantities:

(a) scope and location of the work including extent of work in plant rooms

CLASSIFICATION TABLE

			Unit		MEASUREMENT RULES	DEFINITION RULES	COVERAGE RULES	SUPPLEMENTARY INFORMATION
1 Insulation, type stated	1 Pipelines	1 Nominal size of pipeline stated	m	1 Flanged pipelines 2 Traced oil pipelines 3 Smoke pipelines 4 Flue pipelines	M1 Work related to this Section is classified in accordance with Sections R14 – U70 as Appendix B and given under an appropriate Work Section heading		C1 Insulation is deemed to include: (a) smoothing the materials and working around supports (b) working around pipe flanges (c) working around fittings excluding metal clad facing insulants	S1 Specified under codes of practice and regulations S2 Kind and quality of materials S3 Thickness of materials S4 Coatings and facings S5 Method of fixing
	2 Insulation boxes for pipelines	1 Type of infill stated	nr		M2 Work in plant rooms is identified separately			
	3 Air ductlines	1 Nominal size of ductline stated	m					
	4 Equipment	1 Insulation contained in casings of specific dimensions	m²					
		2 Overall size stated	nr					
2 Items extra over insulation	1 Pipelines	1 Working around ancillaries	nr		M3 Equipment insulation measured superficially is measured on the surface of the insulants			
	2 Air ductlines	2 Boxes for valves, details stated						
	3 Equipment	3 Detachable mattresses			M4 Alternatively items relating to equipment insulation may be given in the description of the enumerated items concerned			
		4 Working around ancillaries						
	4 Pipeline and air ductline fittings where insulation has metal clad facing	5 Details stated						
3 Loose or cellular concrete insulation	1 In trenches, ducts, tank casings and the like	1 Special protection or finish at openings through walls, valve chambers and the like included, details stated	m³					

Y51 Testing and commissioning mechanical services
Y54 Identification - mechanical
Y59 Sundry common mechanical items

159

INFORMATION PROVIDED

P1 Information is shown on location drawings under A Preliminaries/General conditions

CLASSIFICATION TABLE

Classification	Sub-items	Unit	Detail	MEASUREMENT RULES	DEFINITION RULES	COVERAGE RULES	SUPPLEMENTARY INFORMATION
1 Marking position of holes, mortices and chases in the structure	1 Installation stated	item	1 Formed during construction, details stated	M1 Work related to this Section is classified in accordance with Sections R14 – U70 as Appendix B and given under an appropriate Work Section heading			
2 Loose ancillaries	1 Keys 2 Tools 3 Spares 4 Parts/chemicals	nr	1 Name of recipient stated				
3 Identification where not provided with equipment or ancillaries	1 Plates 2 Discs 3 Labels 4 Tapes or bands 5 Arrows, symbols, letters and numbers 6 Charts	nr	1 Type, size and method of fixing stated	1 Details of engraving stated 2 Mounting of charts, details stated			
4 Testing and commissioning	1 Installation stated	item	1 Preparatory operations, details stated 2 Stage tests (nr) listed and purpose stated 3 Insurance Company tests, details stated 4 Instruction of personnel in operation of completed installation	1 Attendance required 2 Instruments to be provided		C1 Provision of water, fuel, gas, electricity and other supplies is deemed to be included C2 Provision of test certificates is deemed to be included	
5 Temporary operation of installations to Employer's requirements	1 Installation and purpose of operation stated	item	1 Duration of operation period stated	1 Attendance required 2 Conditions imposed by Employer before operation allowed 3 Special insurance requirements of Employer stated	M2 Provision of water, fuel, gas, electricity and other supplies is covered by Provisional Sums in Section A54		

6 Preparing drawings	1 Information required and number of copies stated	1 Negatives, prints and microfilms, details stated	item	1 Binding into sets, details stated	D1 Drawings include builder's work, manufacturer's and installation drawings and record or 'as fitted' drawings
				2 Names of recipients stated	
7 Operating and maintenance manuals			item		

Y60 Conduit and cable trunking
Y63 Support components - cables

INFORMATION PROVIDED					MEASUREMENT RULES	DEFINITION RULES	COVERAGE RULES	SUPPLEMENTARY INFORMATION
P1 The following information is shown either on location drawings under A Preliminaries/General conditions or on further drawings which accompany the bills of quantities: (a) scope and location of the work					M1 Work related to these Sections is classified in accordance with Sections V10 – W62 as Appendix B and given under an appropriate Work Section heading	D1 Finishes and surface treatments exclude decorative finishes which are measured under Section M60	C1 Providing everything necessary for jointing is deemed to be included C2 Patterns, moulds, templates and the like are deemed to be included	S1 Specified codes of practice and regulations S2 Kind and quality of materials S3 Gauge thickness or substance of materials S4 Tests with which materials must comply S5 Finishes or surface treatments applied on site S6 Finishes or surface treatments applied off site stating whether applied before or after fabrication or assembly

CLASSIFICATION TABLE

			Unit		MEASUREMENT RULES	DEFINITION RULES	COVERAGE RULES	SUPPLEMENTARY INFORMATION
1 Conduit	1 Straight 2 Curved, radii stated	1 Type and external size and method of fixing stated	m	1 Background stated 2 To surfaces 3 In chases 4 In floor screeds 5 In situ concrete	M2 Conduit is measured over all conduit fittings and branches M3 Independent earth conductors are measured separately under Section Y61 or Y80		C3 Conduit is deemed to include: (a) bending, cutting, screwing, jointing and all conduit fittings excluding 2.*.1.* (b) clips, saddles and crampets (c) forming holes for conduit entry (d) draw wires, draw cables, and the like (e) components for earth continuity	
	3 Flexible connections 4 Extendable connections	1 Type, size, overall length and type of adaptors stated	nr	1 Earthing tails				
2 Items extra over the conduit in which they occur	1 Special boxes 2 Adaptable boxes 3 Floor trap boxes 4 Purpose made boxes 5 Rectangular junction boxes 6 Expansion joints	1 Type, size, cover and method of fixing stated	nr	1 Background stated			C4 Cutting and jointing conduit to boxes is deemed to be included	

Item			Unit		Measurement rules	Coverage rules
3 Connections of conduit to trunking 4 Connections of conduit to equipment and control gear	1 Components 2 Special boxes	1 Type, size and method of jointing stated	nr			
5 Cable trunking	1 Straight 2 Curved, radii stated	1 Type, size, method of jointing and type, spacing and method of fixing supports all stated	m	1 Background stated 2 Pin racks 3 Compartments (nr), size stated	M4 Cable trunking is measured over all fittings and branches M5 Independent earth conductors are measured separately under Sections Y61 and Y80	C5 Trunking is deemed to include components for earth continuity
6 Item extra over the cable trunking in which they occur	1 Fittings	1 Type stated	nr	1 Bushing material, type and size stated		C6 Cutting and jointing trunking to fittings is deemed to be included
7 Connections of cable trunking to equipment and control gear	1 Forming holes 2 With flanges 3 With flanges and forming holes	1 Size of opening stated 2 Size of opening and type and size of flanges stated	nr nr			
8 Cable tray, ladders and racks	1 Straight 2 Curved, radii stated	1 Type, width, method of jointing and type spacing and method of fixing supports, all stated	m	1 Background stated	M6 Cable tray, ladders and racks are measured over all fittings and branches M7 Independent earth conductors are measured separately under Sections Y61 or Y80	C7 Cable tray is deemed to include components for earth continuity
9 Cable tray stools		1 Type and size stated	nr			
10 Items extra over the cable tray, ladders and racks in which they occur	1 Fittings		nr			C8 Cutting and jointing tray to fittings is deemed to be included
11 Supports for cable trunking 12 Supports for cable tray, ladders and racks	1 Supports which differ from those given with the trunking or cable tray, ladders and racks	1 Size of trunking, tray ladder or rack, type and size of support, method of fixing trunking, tray, ladder or rack and support all stated	nr	1 Background stated		

163

Y61   HV/LV cables and wiring
Y62   Busbar trunking
Y80   Earthing and bonding components

INFORMATION PROVIDED	MEASUREMENT RULES	DEFINITION RULES	COVERAGE RULES	SUPPLEMENTARY INFORMATION
P1 The following information is shown either on location drawings under A Preliminaries/General conditions or on further drawings which accompany the bills of quantities: (a) scope and location of the work P2 The following information regarding final circuits is given: (a) a distribution sheet setting out the number and location of all fittings and accessories (b) a location drawing showing the layout of the points				

CLASSIFICATION TABLE

1	2	3	Unit	MEASUREMENT RULES	DEFINITION RULES	COVERAGE RULES	SUPPLEMENTARY INFORMATION
1 Cables	1 Type, size, number of cores, armouring and sheathing stated	1 Drawn into conduits or ducts or laid or drawn into trunking	m	M1 Work related to these Sections is classified in accordance with Sections V10 – W62 as Appendix B and given under an appropriate Work Section heading	D1 Finishes and surface treatments exclude decorative finishes which are deemed to be included measured in Section M60	C1 Providing everything necessary for jointing is deemed to be included	S1 Specified codes of practice and regulations
		1 Type, spacing and method of fixing supports stated		M2 Cables in conduits or trunking and cables fixed to trays are measured as the net length of the conduit, trunking or tray. Other cables are measured as fixed without allowance for sag	D2 Cables are defined as being laced into circuit groups where this is specified	C2 Patterns, moulds, templates and the like are deemed to be included	S2 Kind and quality of materials
		2 Laid or drawn into trunking and laced into circuit groups					S3 Gauge, thickness or substance of materials
		3 Fixed to surfaces		M3 The following allowances shall be made to those cables measured net: (a) 0.30 m on each cable entering fittings, luminaires or accessories (b) 0.60 m on each cable entering equipment or control gear		C3 Cables are deemed to include: (a) wall, floor and ceiling plates (b) cable sleeves (c) connecting tails	S4 Tests with which materials must comply
		2 Background stated					S5 Finishes or surface treatments applied on site
		4 Wrapped around pipework					S6 Finishes or surface treatment applied off site stating whether applied before or after fabrication or assembly
		5 Laid in trenches					S7 Details of colour coding or other markings of cables for phase identification
		6 Fixed to insulators in overhead lines					
		7 Suspended from catenary cables					
2 Flexible cable connections	1 Type, size, number of cores, armouring, sheathing, capacity stated, length ≤ 1.00 m	1 Details of connections at each end stated	nr				
	2 and thereafter in 1.00 m stages						

No.	Item	First division	Second division	Third division	Unit
3	Cable joints	1 Type and size of cable stated	1 Joint boxes, type stated; 2 Sealing boxes, type stated		nr
4	Line taps		1 Shrouds, type stated		nr
5	Cable termination glands	1 Type and size of cable, and type of gland stated	1 Cable connector blocks, type and size stated	1 Box, type, size and method of fixing stated	nr
6	Cable supports which differ from those given with cables	1 Size of cable, type and size of support and method of fixing stated	1 Fixed to surfaces; 2 Fixed to conductors in overhead lines; 3 Suspended from catenary cables		nr
7	Busbar trunking	1 Straight; 2 Curved, radii stated	1 Type, size, cover, method of jointing, number and rated capacity of busbars and type, spacing and method of fixing supports all stated		m
8	Items extra over the busbar trunking in which they occur	1 Fittings	1 Type stated		nr
9	Tap off units	1 Type, size and method of fixing stated	1 Rated capacity stated		nr
10	Feeder units	1 Type, size and method of fixing stated	1 Rated capacity stated		nr
11	Fire barriers	1 Type, size and method of fixing stated			nr
12	Busbar trunking supports which differ from those given with busbar trunking	1 Size of trunking, type and size of support and method of fixing stated			nr
13	Tapes	1 Type and size of tape, type and spacing of fixings and method of fixing stated	1 Background stated		m
14	Connections	1 Type and size of tape, type and spacing of fixings and method of fixing stated	1 Background stated		nr
15	Junctions	1 Type and size of tape stated			nr
16	Test clamps	1 Type, size and method of connecting stated			nr
17	Electrodes	1 Type and size stated	1 Driving into the ground		nr
18	Air termination points	1 Type, size and method of fixing stated	1 Background stated		nr

Measurement rules

M4 Busbar trunking is measured over all fittings and branches

M5 13 – 18.*.0.* are only measured in relation to Section Y80

Coverage rules

C4 Cutting and jointing busbar trunking to fittings, tap off units, feeder units and fire barriers is deemed to be included

C5 Cutting and jointing tapes to connectors, junctions, clamps, electrodes and air termination points is deemed to be included

CLASSIFICATION TABLE

CLASSIFICATION TABLE					MEASUREMENT RULES	DEFINITION RULES	COVERAGE RULES	SUPPLEMENTARY INFORMATION
19 Cable and conduit in final circuits	1 Cable installation, size and type of cable, and description of final circuit stated	1 Sockets, switch sockets and the like	nr	1 Cables and protective conductors for earthing	M6 Final circuits not forming part of a domestic or similar simple installation from distribution boards and the like are kept separate and measured in detail in accordance with Sections Y60 & Y63 and Sections Y61, Y62 & Y80: 1 – 18.*.*.*		C6 Final circuits measured on an enumerated points basis are deemed to include:	S8 Voltage and amperage
		2 Immersion heaters, cooker outlets and the like		2 Special boxes			(a) conduit accessories including conduit boxes required for the particular type of installation	
	2 Cable and conduit installation, size and type of cable and type of conduit, and description of final circuit stated	3 Lighting outlets		3 Surface	M7 Final circuits are measured on an enumerated points basis where they form part of a domestic or similar simple installation from distribution boards and the like		(b) fixing, bending, cutting, screwing and jointing	
		4 One way switches		4 Concealed	M8 Each lighting outlet is measured as one point irrespective of the number of lamps		(c) determining routes	
		5 Two way switches		5 Background and method of fixing stated	M9 Cables and protective conductors for earthing are only given in the description where they form an integral part of the final circuit			
		6 Intermediate switches			M10 Special boxes given in the description are specifically required boxes which differ from those included in C5			

Y70 HV switchgear
Y71 LV switchgear and distribution boards
Y72 Contactors and starters
Y92 Motor drives - electric

INFORMATION PROVIDED

P1 The following information is shown either on location drawings under A Preliminaries/General conditions or on further drawings which accompany the bills of quantities:

(a) scope and location of the work

CLASSIFICATION TABLE

1 Switchgear	1 Type, size, rated capacity and method of fixing stated	1 Cross reference to Specification	nr	1 Fuses
2 Distribution boards				2 Supports provided with the equipment, details and method of fixing stated
3 Contactors and starters				3 Background stated
4 Motor drives	1 Type, size and method of fixing stated		nr	1 Background stated
5 Supports where not provided with switchgear, distribution boards, contactors and starters, or motor drives				

MEASUREMENT RULES	DEFINITION RULES	COVERAGE RULES	SUPPLEMENTARY INFORMATION
M1 Work related to these Sections is classified in accordance with Sections V10 – W62 as Appendix B and given under an appropriate Work Section heading	D1 Finishes and surface treatments exclude decorative finishes which are measured in Section M60	C1 Providing everything necessary for jointing is deemed to be included	S1 Specified codes of practice and regulations
		C2 Patterns, moulds, templates and the like are deemed to be included	S2 Kind and quality of material
		C3 Plates, discs and labels for identification provided with the equipment are deemed to be included	S3 Gauge, thickness or substance of materials
			S4 Tests with which materials must comply
			S5 Finishes or surface treatments applied on site
			S6 Finishes and surface treatments applied off site stating whether applied before or after fabrication or assembly
			S7 Limiting dimensions on the size and weight of the equipment

INFORMATION PROVIDED

P1 The following information is shown either on location drawings under A Preliminaries/General conditions or on further drawings which accompany the bills of quantities:
(a) scope and location of the work

CLASSIFICATION TABLE

			nr	
1 Particular specification items	1 Type and description stated			
2 Luminaires	1 Type, size and method of fixing stated	1 Cross references to Specification	nr	
	2 Pendant, type, size and method of fixing stated	1 Drop ≤ 1.00 m		
		2 Drop > 1.00 m, drop stated		

1 Boxes, details stated
2 Conduit boxes, details stated
3 Pattresses, details stated
4 Ceiling roses, details stated
5 Connector blocks, details stated
6 Flexible cords, details stated
7 Starters, chokes and capacitors, details stated
8 Shades, diffusers and reflectors, details stated
9 Lampholder, details stated
10 Conduit or chain suspension, details stated
11 Suspension system, details stated
12 Lighting columns, details stated
13 Background stated

MEASUREMENT RULES

M1 Work related to these Sections is classified in accordance with Sections V10 – W62 as Appendix B and given under an appropriate Work Section heading

DEFINITION RULES

D1 Finishes and surface treatments exclude decorative finishes which are measured under Section M60

D2 Particular specification items are those items of a fitting or ancillary nature particular to the Work Section concerned

COVERAGE RULES

C1 Providing everything necessary for jointing is deemed to be included

C2 Patterns, moulds, templates and the like are deemed to be included

SUPPLEMENTARY INFORMATION

S1 Specified codes of practice and regulations
S2 Kind and quality of materials
S3 Gauge, thickness or substance of materials
S4 Tests with which materials must comply
S5 Finishes or surface treatments applied on site
S6 Finishes or surface treatments applied off site stating whether applied before or after fabrication or assembly

Item	Description	Supplementary information	Unit	Measurement rules	Coverage rules
3 Lamps	1 Type, size and rated capacity stated		nr	M2 Lamps may alternatively be given in the description of luminaires	C3 Lamps are deemed to include fixing into luminaires
4 Luminaires and lamps provided by the Employer	1 Type, size and method of fixing stated	1 Provision of additional components and internal wiring, details stated 2 Background stated			C4 Accepting delivery, storing and handling are deemed to be included
5 Accessories	1 Type, box and method of fixing stated 1 Rated capacity stated	1 Plugs to be provided with socket outlets 2 Background stated	nr	M3 Accessories are enumerated in gangs where appropriate	C5 Plugs are deemed to include fuses
6 Disconnecting, setting aside and refixing for the convenience of other trades	1 Type of equipment and purpose of disconnection stated		item		

169

Y81 Testing and commissioning electrical services
Y82 Identification - electrical
Y89 Sundry common electrical items

INFORMATION PROVIDED

P1 Information is shown on location drawings under A Preliminaries/General conditions

CLASSIFICATION TABLE

			Unit	Supplementary
1 Additional bonding	1 Bonding resulting from testing extraneous metal		sum	
2 Marking position of holes, mortices and chases in the structure	1 Installation stated		item	1 Formed during construction, details stated
3 Loose ancillaries	1 Keys 2 Tools 3 Spares	1 Type, quality or quantity stated	nr	1 Names of recipients
4 Identification where not provided with equipment or control gear	1 Plates 2 Discs 3 Labels 4 Tapes and bands 5 Arrows, symbols, letters and numbers 6 Charts	1 Type, size and method of fixing stated	item	1 Details of engraving stated 2 Mounting of charts, details stated
5 Testing and commissioning	1 Installation stated	1 Stage tests (nr) listed and purpose stated 2 Instruction of personnel in operation of completed installation	item	1 Attendance required 2 Instruments to be provided
6 Temporary operation of installations, to Employer's requirements	1 Installation and purpose of operation stated	1 Duration of operation period stated	item	1 Attendance required 2 Conditions imposed by Employer before operation allowed 3 Special insurance requirements of Employer stated

MEASUREMENT RULES

M1 Work related to these Sections is classified in accordance with Sections V10 – W62 as Appendix B and given under an appropriate Work Section heading

M2 Alternatively a Provisional Sum may be included in Section A54

M3 Provision of electricity and other supplies is covered by Provisional Sums in Section A54

DEFINITION RULES

COVERAGE RULES

C1 Provision of electricity and other supplies is deemed to be included

C2 Provision of test certificates is deemed to be included

SUPPLEMENTARY INFORMATION

7 Preparing drawings	1 Information required and copies (nr) stated	1 Negatives, prints microfilms, details stated	item	1 Binding into sets, details stated		D1 Drawings include builder's work, installation drawings, and record or 'as fitted' drawings
				2 Names of recipients stated		
8 Operating and maintenance manuals			item			

Work Groups H, J, K, L and M – work to existing buildings

INFORMATION PROVIDED	MEASUREMENT RULES	DEFINITION RULES	COVERAGE RULES	SUPPLEMENTARY INFORMATION
P1 The following information is shown either on location drawings under A Preliminaries/General conditions or on further drawings which accompany the bills of quantities: (a) the scope and location of the work relative to – the existing layout indicating the existing structure – the proposed layout	M1 These rules cover each the work section within the Work Groups H, J, K, L and M and apply to works to existing buildings as defined in the General Rules	D1 Materials arising from work are the property of the Contractor unless otherwise stated	C1 Shoring and scaffolding incidental to the work and making good all work disturbed by such shoring and scaffolding is deemed to be included within each item C2 Items for work to existing buildings are deemed to include: (a) disposal of materials other than those remaining the property of the Employer or those for re-use (b) incidental work which is at the discretion of the Contractor (c) all new fixing or jointing materials required	S1 Method of operation, where by specific means S2 Setting aside and storing materials remaining the property of the Employer or those for re-use S3 Employer's restrictions on methods of disposal of materials including toxic or other special waste S4 Kind, quality and thickness of materials S5 Type of construction S6 Special trims S7 Restrictions on the method of shoring and scaffolding

CLASSIFICATION TABLE

1 Bonding/jointing new to existing	1 Dimensioned description		m²	M3 This item is only measured separately where new work is purely extending the existing	
2 Stripping off/removing/taking down	1 Dimensioned description	1 In preparation for replacement	m² m nr		
	2 Spot item dimensioned description		nr m item		C3 Spot items are deemed to include jointing /bonding new to existing

			Unit		Notes
3 Making good disturbed work	1 Dimensioned description		m²; m; nr	1 To match existing	
	2 Spot item dimensioned description		item		C4 Spot items are deemed to include jointing/bonding new to existing
4 Items extra over making good disturbed work	1 Jointing/bonding new to existing		nr		
5 Cutting	1 Raking		m		
	2 Curved		m		
6 Cutting holes	1 Ducts	1 Girth ≤ 1.00 m 2 Girth 1.00 – 2.00 m 3 and thereafter in 1.00 m stages	nr	1 Rectangular 2 Circular 3 Dimensioned profile description 4 Making good 5 Making good to match existing 6 Facework described	D2 Ducts include trays, trunking, gratings and the like
	2 Pipes	1 ≤ 55 mm nominal size 2 55 – 110 mm nominal size 3 > 110 mm nominal size			D3 Pipes include tubes, bars, cables, conduit and the like

CLASSIFICATION TABLE					MEASUREMENT RULES	DEFINITION RULES	COVERAGE RULES	SUPPLEMENTARY INFORMATION
1 Breaking into existing pipes 2 Breaking into existing ducts	1 Type, size and location of existing pipe or duct stated	1 Purpose of breaking in stated	item	1 Obtaining approval for isolation where necessary 2 Isolating existing pipe or duct 3 Isolating and draining down existing pipe 4 Preparing ends of existing for new work 5 Limitations to shut down period				
3 Jointing new pipes to existing 4 Jointing new ducts to existing	1 Type, size of both pipes or ducts and method of jointing stated		nr	1 Preparing ends of existing pipes and ducts where not taken with 1 – 2.1.1.4		C1 Providing everything necessary for jointing is deemed to be included		
5 Stripping out part installations	1 Dimensioned description detailing extent and location 2 Spot item dimensioned description		nr item	1 Obtaining approval for isolation where necessary 2 Isolating part or whole to be removed 3 Isolating and draining down part or whole to be rescued 4 Making safe 5 Limitations to shut down period				
6 Stripping out whole installations	1 Dimensioned description		nr					
7 Provision of temporary services, bypasses and the like	1 Dimensioned description		nr	1 Fabrication prior to installation	M1 Alternatively this work may be measured in accordance with the Rules for new work and grouped under an appropriate heading		C2 Provision of temporary services, bypasses and the like is deemed to include removing and making good after	
8 Stripping off insulation to part of services installations	1 Dimensioned description detailing extent and location 2 Spot item dimensioned description	1 Type of insulation to be removed	nr item	1 Safety measures to be applied 2 Disposal requirements				
9 Stripping off insulation to whole services installations								

| 10 Testing and commissioning existing plumbing and mechanical installations | 1 Part installation stated
2 Whole installation stated | item

1 Preparatory operations, details stated
2 Stage tests (nr) listed and purpose stated
3 Insurance Company tests, if any, details stated
4 Instruction of personnel in operation of completed installation | item

1 Attendance required
2 Instruments to be provided
3 Special insurance requirements of Employer stated | C3 Provision of water, fuel, gas, electricity and other supplies is deemed to be included
C4 Provision of test certificates is deemed to be included |

CLASSIFICATION TABLE					MEASUREMENT RULES	DEFINITION RULES	COVERAGE RULES	SUPPLEMENTARY INFORMATION
1 Cables drawn into existing conduits or ducts or laid or drawn in existing trunking	1 Type, size, number of cores, armouring and sheathing stated		m		M1 Except for final circuits cables in conduits or trunking and cables fixed to trays are measured as the net length of the conduit, trunking or tray. Other cables are measured as fixed without allowance for sag M2 The following allowances shall be made: (a) 0.30 m on each cable entering fittings, luminaires or accessories (b) 0.60 m on each cable entering equipment or control gear	D1 Cables are defined as being laced into circuit groups only where this is specified	C1 Cables and tapes are deemed to include: (a) wall, floor and ceiling plates (b) cable sleeves C2 Cables laid or drawn into existing conduits, existing ducts or existing trunking is deemed to include removing and replacing existing covers, existing inspection lids and the like C3 Providing everything necessary for jointing is deemed included	S1 Details of colour coding or other markings of cables for phase identification
2 Cables laid or drawn into existing trunking and laced into circuit groups	1 Type and size of existing conduit or duct stated 2 Type and size of existing trunking stated							
3 Breaking into existing cables	1 Type, size and location of existing cable, equipment or control gear stated	1 Purpose of breaking in stated, details of associated conduit, trunking or tray given	nr	1 Obtaining approval to isolation where necessary 2 Isolating existing cable, equipment or control gear 3 Preparing existing for joining of new work				
4 Breaking into existing equipment and control gear			nr					
5 Jointing new cables to existing	1 Type, size of both new and existing work and method of jointing stated		nr	1 Preparing existing for jointing to new where not taken with 3-4.1.1.3 2 Joint boxes, type stated 3 Sealing boxes, type stated 4 Shrouds, type stated 5 Boxes, type stated 6 Special boxes, type stated 7 Other components, type stated				
6 Jointing new equipment and control gear to existing								
7 Jointing new conduits, trunking and trays to existing								
8 Stripping out part installations	1 Dimensioned description detailing extent and location		nr	1 Obtaining approval for isolation where necessary 2 Isolating whole or part to be removed 3 Making safe 4 Limitations to shut down period				
9 Stripping out whole installations	2 Spot item dimensioned description		item					

	First division	Second division	Third division	Unit	Measurement/Coverage rules
10 Provision of temporary services	1 Dimensioned description			nr	C4 Provision of temporary services is deemed to include removing and making good after C5 Provision of electricity and other supplies is deemed to be included C6 Provision of test certificates is deemed to be included
11 Testing and commissioning existing electrical installations	1 Part installation stated 2 Whole installation stated	1 Stage tests (nr) listed and purpose stated 2 Instruction of personnel in operation of completed installation	1 Attendance required 2 Instruments to be provided 3 Special insurance requirements of Employer stated	item	M3 Alternatively this work may be measured in accordance with the rules for new work and grouped under an appropriate heading

Appendix A

Fixtures, furnishings, equipment, fittings and appliances as referred to in the rules for Work Sections N10, N11, N12, N13, N15, N20-N23, P21 and Q50

N10 General fixtures/furnishings/equipment

Furnishings, fittings and equipment, fixed to the building fabric or provided loose within the building, and 'general' in the sense that they may be found in a wide variety of buildings. Culinary and sanitary furnishings, fittings and equipment are excluded, together with items which would normally be included in building services sub-contracts. Minor items of special purpose equipment may be included here rather than in sections N20–N23 'Special purpose fixtures/furnishings/equipment'.

Included

Counters, desks, benches, worktops

Small mirrors in toilets, dressing rooms

Curtain track and rails

Curtains, loose wall hangings, fabrics, blinds

Fireplaces, surrounds and hearths

Telephone booths and enclosures

Storage racks, shelves, shelving support systems

Door mats, matwells

Wall hangings, loose carpets

Lockers, hat and coat rails

General purpose chairs and tables

Beds, divans

Wardrobes, dressers, cupboards, cabinets

Objets d'art and other ornamental features

Fire extinguishers

Dustbins

Minor items of 'special purpose' equipment

Fixing as required

N11 Domestic kitchen fittings

Domestic kitchen equipment of all kinds including units, worktops, cupboards, sinks, cookers, grills, refrigerators, etc.

Included

Kitchen units, including base units, drawer units, worktops, hanging cupboards

Ovens, cookers, hobs, grills

Sinks, taps, waste fittings, waste disposal units where supplied as part of the kitchen fitting installation.

Refrigerators, deep freezers

Dishwashers

Clothes washing machines, clothes dryers, ironing cabinets

Waste bins, towel rails, storage racks and other accessories

Kitchen equipment suites comprising any combination of the foregoing

Fixing

N12 Catering Equipment

Culinary equipment designed for use in provision of food and drink on a communal or commercial scale.

Included

Food storage equipment other than cold rooms

Food preparation and cooking equipment

Food transporting and serving equipment

Serving counters and tray rails

Sinks where supplied as part of the catering equipment installation

Dishwashing and waste disposal equipment

Food and drink vending machines

Fixing

N13 Sanitary appliances/fittings

Appliances for health, hygiene and personal washing, together with their accessories, but excluding sinks for domestic kitchens.

Included

Low level WC suites
WC pans and cisterns
Slop hoppers
Urinals and cisterns
Sinks, including kitchen sinks not supplied as part of the kitchen fitting installation, and catering sinks not supplied as part of the catering equipment installation
Wash basins
Hand rinse basins
Wash fountains
Bidets
Baths
Jacuzzis
Showers including curtain rails, screens, etc.
Drinking fountains
Vanity units
Taps and waste fittings to the appliances
Float operated valves
Bath panels and trim
Hand dryers
Towel rails and holders not connected to a heating or hot water supply installation
Paper towel dispensers
Toilet paper holders
Waste bins
Soap dispensers and holders
Sanitary towel incinerators
Sanitary towel macerators
Saunas, sauna equipment

N15 Signs/Notices

Directories, notice boards, letters, signs, plaques, symbols and emblems of all kinds for identification and directional purposes.

Included

Signwriting
Lettering, emblems and other identification/directional symbols carved onto stone
Door or floor numbering or lettering
Name plates, plaques and identification symbols of all materials
Directional signboards and notice boards of all kinds and materials
Shop front lettering, emblems and symbols of all kinds and materials
Illuminated signs, lettering, emblems and symbols such as "Exit" signs, "Gentlemen", etc. where the illuminated fitting is simply connected to an adjacent electrical outlet

N20 – N23 Special purpose fixtures/ furnishings/equipment

Furnishings, fittings and equipment, fixed to the building or provided loose within the building, and 'special' in the sense that they are designed for the particular purpose(s) of the building. The title(s) of the section(s) should indicate the nature of the special purpose equipment, e.g. 'Special purpose hospital fixtures/ furnishings/equipment'. Section titles will therefore vary from project to project. Four work section numbers have been allocated to provide for projects with several types of special purpose fixtures, furnishings and equipment.

General purpose, residential, culinary and sanitary fixtures, fittings and equipment are excluded, together with items which would normally be included in building services sub-contracts. Minor items of special purpose equipment may be included in section N10 'General fixtures/ furnishings/equipment' rather than here.

Included

Fixtures, fittings and equipment for special purposes, including:
Rail, road, water and air transport buildings
Communications, power supply, mineral supply, water supply buildings
Agricultural, fishing and forestry buildings
Factories and other industrial buildings for food, drink, chemicals, engineering, textiles, clay, cement, timber, construction, etc.
Administrative, office and commercial buildings
Shops, showrooms, stores, shopping centres, warehouses
Defence, police, prison and fire service buildings
Hospital, medical, welfare and animal welfare buildings
Restaurants, snack bars, public houses
Entertainment buildings, community centres, clubs
Sports buildings, swimming pools, marinas, stadia
Religious buildings, funerary buildings
Educational buildings including scientific research facilities
Libraries, record offices, museums, galleries, zoos
Special residential buildings, hotels, old peoples' homes

P21 Ironmongery

Components and items of metal, plastics or other material fixed on site as door and window opening or closing devices, fasteners, supports, brackets, etc. but excluding

1. Items supplied with a window or other component.
2. Items of furniture or equipment in their own right (e.g. towel rails, toilet roll holders).

Included

Water bars

Sliding and up and over door tracks or overhead rails; hangers, guides and fittings

Sash balances

Butts, hinges, pivots and other opening/closing devices

Spring butts, door springs, door closers and other self closing devices

Locks, latches, catches, cylinder locks, nightlatches and other locking devices

Bolts, panic bolts, espagnolette bolts, security bolts, casement and sash fasteners and other securing devices

Door handles, escutcheons, casement stays, sash pulls, letter plates, kicking plates, push plates, pull handles, trickle ventilators and other door and window furniture

Shelf brackets other than part of a shelving system

Handrail brackets

Door stops, retaining devices, draughtproofing strips and sections

Nameplates, numbers, knockers, bell pushes, door viewers

Mechanical and/or automatic operating or opening equipment where not supplied with the component or installed as part of an access control installation

Q50 Site/Street furniture/equipment

General purpose furniture and equipment of any material designed for use externally, but excluding items provided by a statutory undertaker, local authority or services sub-contractor.

Included

Gates (when not part of fencing), including lifting barriers

Pedestrian and vehicle barriers and railings

Bollards (including removable and collapsible)

Prefabricated plant containers

Seats, benches, tables

Litter bins, grit bins, dust bins

Poster display units

Cycle stands

Flag staffs

Clothes drying fittings

Sculptures and other ornamental features

Sports and playground equipment

Other special purpose equipment occuring externally

Excavation, concrete backfilling for foundations

Appendix B

Classification of mechanical and electrical services as referred to in the rules for Work Group Y

R Disposal systems

R14 Laboratory/Industrial waste drainage
R20 Sewage pumping
R21 Sewage treatment/sterilisation
R30 Centralised vacuum cleaning
R31 Refuse chutes
R32 Compactors/Macerators
R33 Incineration plant

S Piped supply systems

S10 Cold water
S11 Hot water
S12 Hot and cold water (small scale)
S13 Pressurised water
S14 Irrigation
S15 Fountains/Water features
S20 Treated/Deionised/Distilled water
S21 Swimming pool water treatment
S30 Compressed air
S31 Instrument air
S32 Natural gas
S33 Liquid petroleum gas
S34 Medical/Laboratory gas
S40 Petrol/Oil – lubrication
S41 Fuel oil storage/distribution
S50 Vacuum
S51 Steam
S60 Fire hose reels
S61 Dry risers
S62 Wet risers
S63 Sprinklers
S64 Deluge
S65 Fire hydrants
S70 Gas fire fighting
S71 Foam fire fighting

T Mechanical heating/Cooling/Refrigeration systems

T10 Gas/Oil fired boilers
T11 Coal fired boilers
T12 Electrode/Direct electric boilers
T13 Packaged steam generators
T14 Heat pumps
T15 Solar collectors
T16 Alternative fuel boilers
T20 Primary heat distribution
T30 Medium temperature hot water heating
T31 Low temperature hot water heating
T32 Low temperature hot water heating (small scale)
T33 Steam heating
T40 Warm air heating
T41 Warm air heating (small scale)
T42 Local heating units
T50 Heat recovery
T60 Central refrigeration plant
T61 Primary/Secondary cooling distribution
T70 Local cooling units
T71 Cold rooms
T72 Ice pads

U Ventilation/Air conditioning systems

U10 General supply/extract
U11 Toilet extract
U12 Kitchen extract
U13 Car parking extract
U14 Smoke extract/Smoke control
U15 Safety cabinet/Fume cupboard extract
U16 Fume extract
U17 Anaesthetic gas extract
U20 Dust collection
U30 Low velocity air conditioning
U31 VAV air conditioning
U32 Dual-duct air conditioning
U33 Multi-zone air conditioning
U40 Induction air conditioning
U41 Fan-coil air conditioning
U42 Terminal re-heat air conditioning
U43 Terminal heat pump air conditioning
U50 Hybrid system air conditioning
U60 Free standing air conditioning units
U61 Window/Wall air conditioning units
U70 Air curtains

V Electrical supply/power lighting systems

V10 Electricity generation plant
V11 HV supply/distribution/public utility supply
V12 LV supply/public utility supply
V20 LV distribution
V21 General lighting
V22 General LV power
V30 Extra low voltage supply
V31 DC supply
V32 Uninterrupted power supply
V40 Emergency lighting
V41 Street/Area/Flood lighting
V42 Studio/Auditorium/Arena lighting
V50 Electric underfloor heating
V51 Local electric heating units
V90 General lighting and power (small scale)

W Communications/Security/ Control systems

W10 Telecommunications
W11 Staff paging/location
W12 Public address/Sound amplification
W13 Centralized dictation
W20 Radio/TV/CCTV
W21 Projection
W22 Advertising display
W23 Clocks
W30 Data transmission
W40 Access control
W41 Security detection and alarm
W50 Fire detection and alarm
W51 Earthing and bonding
W52 Lightning protection
W53 Electromagnetic screening
W60 Monitoring
W61 Central control
W62 Building automation

Alphabetical Index

X

No entries

Y

No entries

Z

Zinc sheet coverings/flashings